YOUR SALES CAREER STRATEGY

AN INSIDER'S GUIDE TO THOSE CONSIDERING A CAREER IN OUTSIDE SALES

CHRIS GILMORE

Copyright © 2007 Christopher E. Gilmore

ISBN: 1-4196-6711-4
ISBN-13: 978-1419667114
Library of Congress Control Number: 2007903024

Visit www.booksurge.com to order additional copies.

For permission requests and special book orders, please contact the author through the contact information section of his website: www.salescareerstrategy.com

Back cover photo of the author by Abby Hathaway
Cover and graphics designed by Heather Francis, PrintManagement, www.printmgmt.com

VALUE PROPOSITION TO THE READER

The *value proposition** for this book is to help prevent bad career decisions and maximize your career satisfaction by leveraging advice from real-world experience and research. If the book is successful in achieving this goal, and this book saves you just one "job hop," your savings from that one bad move could amount to thousands of dollars of income and days, months, and possibly, years of career detours and frustration.

This is a guidebook for those with a strong desire or at least an interest in researching careers as *outside salespeople.** They want to avoid starting in the wrong industry, company, or sales position. In other words, they make the right professional career decisions but not the correct job choices.

The subject matter covered includes:

- Why Sales as a Career for You?
- What Sales Job is for You?
  - Industry
  - Company
  - Sales position
- Analyzing Sales Job Offers
  - Sales compensation plans
  - Legal issues with sales positions
- What You Need to Know
  - Important sales terms when interviewing*
  - Recommended reading
- The Checklist for Your Career Strategy

---

* *Chapter 7 is a glossary of necessary sales and business terms for salespeople. Those terms used in the book will appear in bold and italics as illustrated above.*

PREFACE

Joke: What do you call a person who can't find steady employment?

Answer: Consultant

In reading about all of my experiences in *Your Sales Career Strategy*, you may think I am a consultant. Actually, I am gainfully employed as a national account executive and working in the healthcare sector managing a multimillion-dollar sales territory. I am very happy with my industry, company, and position. However, my friend and trusted advisor, Dr. Dave (Dr. David W. Rosenthal, Farmer School of Business, Miami University), cautioned me that I might have a problem with my credibility since readers will realize quickly that I have had a unique and rare career path that has spanned six different industries and companies over fifteen years.

That is what I have always liked about Dr. Dave. He tells you to your face what he thinks, even if it might hurt a little. In this case, it did not hurt because I had already been grinding over the same issue myself. How do I convey that I am a "subject matter expert" who is connected to a host of selling environments that are changing every nanosecond and not a job hopper who has not acquired any meaningful professional experience? We concluded that I needed to tell my story.

The opposite of me would be salespeople who have had the same sales position since they graduated from college or high school. Those salespeople would not have the variety of experiences and perspectives to write this book. I have been very blessed in that four of the six company career changes for me were opportunities that appeared without my solicitation. In three of the four situations, I had to put together my resume after the owners had already made me a verbal offer. The resume was simply for the human resource department's file. My first job out of college and my dot. com termination were the only two instances where I had to go out and find a position out of necessity. In my sales roles, I have been very fortunate in that I have grown every territory's sales volume. Additionally, five of the six companies thought enough of me to offer me a promotion by title and/or responsibility.

Ever since I knocked on my first doors as a paperboy collecting the monthly subscriptions in grade school, I knew I wanted to be in sales. I wrote this book to be the reference book that I never had when I began researching and building my own sales career strategy. It is with great excitement that I offer the information in this book, which I hope you will use to achieve a happy, long, and successful career in sales.

Chris Gilmore

www.salescareerstrategy.com

TABLE OF CONTENTS

DEDICATION

"Teamwork is working together—even when apart."

— Unknown

I would like to thank and acknowledge all those family members, friends, educators, customers, prospects, bosses, and coworkers who, knowingly or unknowingly, have helped me form my philosophies, morals, and beliefs that are a part of this book and me. A special thank you goes to my friends Matt Scherocman and Dr. David W. Rosenthal for spending their extra time and intellect editing the content and sharing candid comments for improving this book.

Specifically, I want to thank those who helped make this book possible. My wife, Anne, offered me encouragement when she could have doubted me, which was instrumental for me finishing this eight-year odyssey. My first teachers, my mother and father, were instrumental in sending me down the initial path that anything was possible. To my boys, this book proves you can do *anything* you put your mind to.

INTRODUCTION

"You can have everything in life that you want if you
will just help other people get what they want."

– Zig Ziglar

Why did I write this book? This book is for people who have an interest in becoming salespersons, and are looking for an insider's insight into how to pursue a sales career in a logical way. Zig has it right. I want to help you by leveraging my years of direct selling experience, in addition to years of consulting and research of many different sales roles, companies, and industries. Specifically, this book is for two types of people:

- Those people who have a high interest in becoming an *outside sales representative*, but have never been in that role.

- Salespeople who are not satisfied with their current sales position and are looking for strategic advice from an experienced salesperson before they change sales positions or decide to leave the sales profession altogether.

Please note that there are many outstanding books and tapes to help people with their sales techniques and "tricks" to become better or more successful salespeople. However, this is NOT one of those books (see Chapter 8 for some of my favorites).

The Inspiration for the Book

Many years ago, the idea for this book came to me in my mobile office. You know . . . my car. This is where most salespeople create, plan, and strategize. At that specific moment, I was analyzing why the first person I had ever hired as a salesperson had just resigned with only three months under his belt. It made me reflect back on my expectations and preconceptions of what *outside sales* would be like before I had any sales experience.

At that time, the owners of the company had recently promoted me to sales manager. The first thing I needed to do was hire a salesperson to replace me in the territory that I was vacating. I made the decision to hire "Wilson." He was my first choice. Wilson had all the attributes needed for selling our products. Wilson was a customer who was also an engineer, and I personally helped educate him on our products. Wilson routinely selected our products for his clients' projects because he believed in the value and quality of the products. Even with his extensive technical experience and outstanding educational background, Wilson's most impressive traits were his persuasive personality and his enthusiasm to become a salesperson. Even before I became the sales manager, he routinely asked how he could work for us and make "the big bucks" in sales.

Wilson decided to quit the job and return to the same job and engineering company that he previously described as "boring and monotonous" after only three months in training and in sales. During his exit interview, I asked Wilson what he was going to take away from his short time in sales. He confessed that sales was more difficult than he thought and he was making a financial mistake by not sticking with it.

Wilson might have made a different decision if he were a part of Generation Next (eighteen to twenty-five-year-olds). In a 2007 survey, the Pew Research Center found that 81 percent of Generation Next said that getting rich is their generation's first or second most important goal in life. However, at that time, it became clear to me that we had to reevaluate the characteristics and traits we were looking for in a salesperson. Sometimes it's not enough to have an outgoing personality, be money motivated, and believe in the product that you are selling.

It was apparent to me that sales was more than a job. It might be the reason why many companies have difficulty filling sales positions. A 2006

Manpower Inc. (NYSE: MAN) survey of nearly 33,000 employers across twenty-three countries and territories found that sales representative jobs were the most difficult positions in the world to fill. The United States was no exception since it, too, ranked sales as the hardest position to fill. Therefore, it takes the right combination of attitude, personality, determination, motivation, and intellect for job satisfaction *and* success to occur.

During my career, I have had many mentors from whom I sought advice when I was thinking about career changes and strategies. I have been very fortunate in that 99 percent of the career advice that my mentors provided was the correct advice. Of all the guidance, the best advice was "You've gotta to look out for number one (YOU) because no one else will." It is a harsh statement, but it is true. Even the people who love, admire, and respect you cannot manage your professional career. YOU have to make the decisions and weigh your options that will help you reach your career aspirations and potential.

What Is the *"Return on Investment"* for This Book?

With every purchase made, the buyer, knowingly or unknowingly calculates a **Return on Investment (ROI)**. This book is no exception to this rule. You picked it up or reviewed it online and asked yourself, "Why should I read this?" It could have been the cover or the catchy title that caught your eye, or simply your online search parameters. But what moved you to purchase it and read it up to this point? This is a nonfiction book, so there is some perceived value by you to read it.

The *value proposition** for this book is to prevent bad career decisions and maximize your career satisfaction leveraging advice that is based on "real world" experience and research.

If the book is successful in achieving this goal and this book saves you just one "job hop," the savings from that one bad move could amount to thousands of dollars of income and days, months, and possibly, years of career detours and frustration for you.

From a company's perspective, hiring a salesperson who does not "turn over" is very important. They understand that employee turnover costs them a lot of money as well. Companies place different values on this cost. One approximation used by many companies is 1.5 times salary.

Value of This Book

Intro. I

Assume:
- **$50,000** - Cost of changing one job
- **$20.00** - What your time is worth now
- **10 Hours** - The time it takes you to read this book
- **$200.00** - Opportunity Costs ($20 x 10 hours)
- **$16.95** - The price you paid for this book

Return on Investment Method (ROI)

$$\frac{\text{Money saved from Job Hopping} - \text{Opportunity Cost of Reading the Book} - \text{Cost of the Book}}{\text{Cost of the Book} + \text{Opportunity Cost of Reading the Book}} = ROI$$

$$\frac{\$50,000 - \$200 - \$16.95}{\$200 + \$16.95} = 22947\%$$

OR

Value Method

$$\begin{array}{l}\text{Money saved from Job Hopping} \\ - \text{Opportunity Cost of Reading the Book} \\ - \text{Cost of the Book}\end{array}$$

$$= \textbf{VALUE}$$

$50,000.00
- $200.00
- $16.95

$49,783.05 of Value

That factor includes recruiting, relocation, and training a replacement employee. If the average salary for a white-collar employee is $45,000 per year, it would mean that the average expense for one employee to leave is around $67,500 for the employer!

From a salesperson's perspective, "job hopping" can be even more expensive! For the *ROI* illustration, we will take the amount of *opportunity cost* (time you could be doing something other than reading this book) and add that to the commissions that you lose by leaving your old sales job and the loss of commissions as you "ramp up" into your new job. You divide all of that by the cost of this book to get your *ROI* for this book.

What Sales Advice Do I Give?

As I mentioned, this is not a selling techniques book, but I do have three important, yet simple, pieces of advice for people starting out in sales.

The first rule is simply the "The Golden Rule" - treat others as you wish to be treated. It is my focus in life and it is my philosophy in business. It seems obvious, but it is still hard for many people to follow.

A second piece of advice is to think like a business owner when managing your sales efforts. The best salespeople view their territory as their own small business or franchise. They write a business plan every year and are constantly aware of their personal "brand." They make sure it is sending the right message and are always building it every day. Likewise, they take ownership of the goods and services that they are selling all the while they are keeping their customers' needs in perspective.

Last bit of advice is to work hard and be prepared. As Woody Allen, the Academy Award-winning director and writer said, "Eighty percent of success is showing up." Be good at showing up on time, ready to "do business." The remaining twenty percent is the sweat that separates you from your peers and competition. It still amazes me how so many sales-people fail at this.

In summary, there are a lot reasons why people pursue a career in sales. From this book, you will see how a seasoned sales professional strategically evaluates and analyzes industries, companies, and sales positions. Other chapters will cover compensation packages, legal issues, important sales terms, and recommended books for reading. All of this leads us back to the question, "Why do YOU want to be in sales?" Is it the money, lifestyle, image, or the business experience in sales that attracts you?

SECTION I – WHY SALES AS A CAREER FOR YOU?

CHAPTER 1 – IS SALES FOR YOU?

"Of those to whom much is given, much is required."

– Luke 12:48 as paraphrased by John F. Kennedy

If I heard it once, I heard it a thousand times. "I wish I were in sales . . . you guys make all the money." I bite my lip. It is the most envied position in the corporate world. Frequently, managers who were "promoted" out of sales wish they were in sales again while many others in an organization wish they had an opportunity to become salespeople.

Personally, I can understand why non-salespeople are envious of salespeople. Aside from running the company, I could not imagine doing anything else in any organization. It is my belief that the best salespeople act like a "small business owner" without the ownership responsibility and risk. In essence, the salespeople are hedging their financial risk by outsourcing a lot of the small business headaches and hassles (i.e., finding and managing employees, employee benefits, accounting compliance, financial concerns, and real estate issues) to the company. The company assumes those issues so the salespeople can drive sales revenue for the company and income for themselves.

The ownership mentality results in salespeople who make smart choices and conduct themselves professionally. They spend the company's money as if it were their own and make efficient use of their time. This ownership mentality of salespeople is the reason that the majority of the CEOs and business owners were involved with sales at one point in their careers. If you don't have this "small business owner" mentality, you won't be a high performer, and you won't be in sales long.

Let's pause for a moment to question: "Why do companies hire salespeople?" They want more gross sales, and more importantly—profit. There is constant pressure on the business owners and sales managers to "grow the business." Therefore, they develop extravagant (or simple in some cases) compensation plans to reward salespeople who bring in and maintain profitable deals and clients. The compensation plans all have the same conclusion: "Produce and be rewarded." For sales growth and profits to occur, three things could happen without changing the existing *business model* and product mix. First, the company can raise prices. Second, the sales manager can apply "the whip" (or offer more "carrots") to the existing sales staff. The third option is simply to add more salespeople.

Early in my career, I was selling for a Fortune 500 company. I had built a strong relationship with a customer who was the VP of sales for his company and who was an active entrepreneur outside of his sales responsibilities. When we were out to lunch one day, he put the importance of salespeople into perspective for me. He challenged me to name any for-profit product or service (or nonprofit, for that matter) that did not need a salesperson involved in the sale of that product or service. Hint: There isn't one. That simple idea will be a constant…forever. No, the Internet will not replace the need for salespeople. In fact, the U.S. Department of Labor recently showed the sales profession growing at the rate of thirty-three percent by the year 2010 (www.bls.gov).

A toothpick was the product that jumped into my mind when he challenged me to name a product. We were at the cash register of the restaurant at the time, and it was the first thing that I saw. But, as I thought about it, even a product as simple as a toothpick, has a variety of salespeople calling on the toothpick manufacturer to keep them "pumping out" toothpicks. Salespeople are providing lumber, toothpick machining equipment, packaging, insurance, and uniforms for the workers at the plant. These "supply chain" salespeople are just helping the toothpick salespeople sell more toothpicks to the retailers. So, can we agree that salespeople have an important role in every company's success?

This book is a guide to those who have a strong desire or interest to be in sales, but want to avoid starting in the wrong industry, company, or position. In other words, you make the right professional decision (sales) but not the correct job choice because of the industry, company, and/or position. For this to book to be beneficial and make the best use of your time, we must first understand the factors that drive people toward sales as a profession. You can perform your own self-evaluation to see how you prioritize these factors.

Money Motivated?

Money is a motivating factor for most people interested in a career in sales. It is an important requirement but not an absolute. Many successful salespeople love what they do and take great pride in servicing their customers and clients. The money that they make is a result of their passion.

However, would you want a salesperson who is motivated by money if you owned a business? That answer would be an emphatic "YES"! The reason for this is that the more the salesperson makes, the more money the company makes (if the compensation plans is set up correctly). For this reason, you should not shy away from being money motivated in interviews for sales positions. The running joke for sales managers is to hire salespeople with big mortgages and expensive cars since those people have the most motivation to sell.

The fine line that salespeople must walk is that money motivation should not be obvious to the point of desperation in dealing with clients and prospects. Buyers do not like greedy salespeople looking for a quick buck. They want salespeople who LISTEN, understand their needs, provide solutions to their business needs, and follow up (do what they say they are going to do). Buyers see through people trying to "put one over on them" or people who do not have a sense of professional pride. In essence, customers must TRUST the salesperson knows what they need and will service them as promised.

In summary, money is a major factor that drives successful salespeople. The more salespeople focus on servicing their clients' needs, the greater the chances are that the salespeople will attain their financial goals. However, even the best intentions to focus on customers' needs can be seen as greed in their eyes.

Stories from the Road: #1

Real-world Lesson: Your customer's perceptions are reality (no matter what your intentions are).

I first learned this lesson early in my career when I was involved with a fast-moving project. Our company specialized in the piping that the project used and we provided our knowledge to our customers at no charge. The engineer I was working with was an employee of a multinational petroleum company that needed the piping product at their Toledo, Ohio, plant within six weeks of my call.

Consumed by this project, I worked with the engineer for weeks with multiple phone calls and e-mails to make sure the piping system would be properly sized with the correct fittings for the project. The problem was that the pipe diameter and wall thickness were a nonstandard size for production, and this would be considered a special order. When the project was finally designed and with budget approval, the exact piping product was on a production "run" from another job. It was the only pipe extruder in our system that could handle a diameter that big. If the order was not placed during that production run, we would lose the order to our main competitor because it would be at least a month before it could be produced because of their current backlog of orders and retooling issues. My engineer contact in Toledo told me to coordinate the order through a purchasing agent I had never spoken to who was in Houston, Texas.

When I called the purchasing agent, I explained that I had been working with the engineer in Toledo. As delicately as I could, I also told him that I would need a *purchase order number* from him within twenty-four hours to keep our place in the production line and meet the project delivery time frame. Since the total dollar amount of the project was over $100,000, the purchasing agent's perception, which he gladly shared with me, was that I was trying to "hot box" him (pressure him into making a quick decision). I lost the order to our competition. In following up with the contractor who was awarded the project, he said that it took him six weeks to get the piping product, which delayed completion of the project.

In summary, the buyer's perception is (and it will always be) reality. The valuable sales lesson I learned from that lost order was to verify and understand how the buying process would be on all future projects. In advance of spending too much time on "free" consulting with the engineer, I was able to better qualify the possibilities of winning the business by talking to the procurement people.

Is it the Lifestyle?

How many positions in any company give you an expense account with an entertainment budget? How many jobs pay you to make new friends and meet leaders in business? How about a car allowance or a company car? How about the freedom to set your own schedule? Not every sales job offers those same perks, but most *outside sales* positions do.

The "career lifestyle" of taking clients golfing and to lunch and developing friendships is something that motivates many people to pursue a career in sales. It certainly did for me. You have been empowered with the "keys" to drive the business. There are many means to an end for delivering sales, and the expense account is one tool that salespeople enjoy using.

What many people with "sales rep lifestyle envy" do not realize is the "after hours" work and travel that is a part of a career in sales. Successful salespeople might be golfing with clients during business hours, but they know that their paperwork and a "quota" still await them when they get back to the office, hotel, or their home that night. Successful salespeople understand this and prioritize their time by spending their nights and weekends working on the "B" tasks. They spend business hours on "A" tasks such as communicating and meeting with clients and prospects. Additionally, one phone call can reprioritize your business and personal "to do" list for you that day or night if you need to get a proposal out the next day. That is why I consider it a lifestyle decision and not just a job decision. You are always "on."

Early in my career someone made an analogy between sales representatives and "desperadoes." They are the voice and brand of the organization that they represent. They are cowboys and cowgirls out on their own, "riding" from one customer, client, and prospect to another. They are very solitary but resourceful. Although crude, this analogy is fitting and true. Salespeople travel and "cold call" prospects looking for business by themselves. Many sales representatives work out of their homes, further increasing this feeling of isolation. A phone and a prospect list become your only "friends" on many days. This self-starter independence is something that all salespeople must accept and embrace.

Traveling is another lifestyle consideration for people interested in sales. It might be obvious, but traveling is a must for most salespeople. Driving, flying, and "overnighting" on a moment's notice can be a perk for some people; for others it is a deciding factor when considering a sales job. The stress of traveling can be enormous on a family structure. Wives, husbands, children, and significant others have a hard time understanding a constant travel schedule that many salespeople must maintain. It is worth mentioning that many business owners and sales managers want their salespeople to maintain "normal" life-work balance. The last thing they want to promote is constant "burnout" of their salespeople, which causes turnover and more issues in recruiting and hiring new salespeople. However, not all sales positions require extensive travel. There are some industries where salespeople cover small geographic territories that do not even require overnight travel (see **Stories from the Road – #2**).

It is important to know your tolerance for travel when you begin your search and when you start to interview. You should understand that outside sales, by definition, requires some travel. Although travel is a constant, the degree and the type (airplane and/or car) of travel that is required will vary greatly for each position, company, and industry.

Stories from the Road – #2

Real-world Lesson: Not all sales jobs require extensive travel.

While most sales positions require extensive travel, some do not require even overnight travel. In general, pharmaceutical, printing sales, and medical sales are examples of positions that require very little overnight travel.

In the management of my own career, I have been fortunate to accept only positions that met my needs: money, experience, family/work balance. Money and experience are the key components of what you need from your work while your time with your family counterbalances the time spent working and traveling. Below is a dramatized graph that illustrates how a salesperson can lose income with travel restrictions while balancing a changing family life.

Travel Flexibility Curve Tendencies

1.1

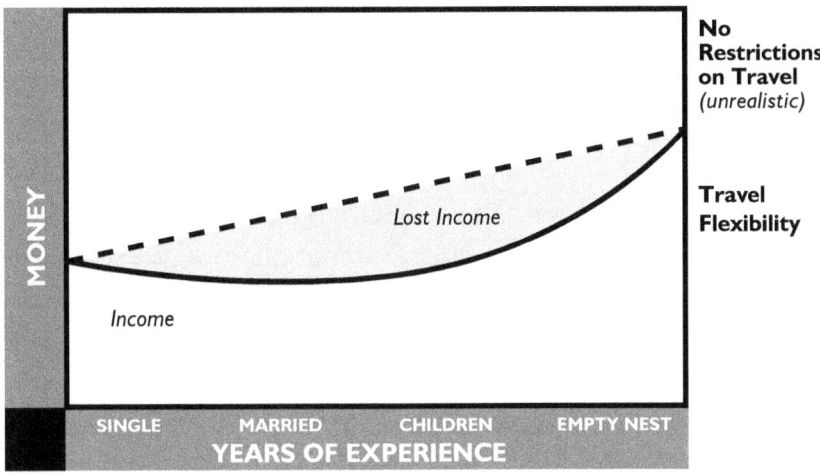

The Prestige of Being a Leader

Can prestige be a reason to pursue a sales career? YES! Although many people in companies admit they could not be in sales because it is difficult, many more wish they could be in sales. Any time people wish they could be doing what you are doing, prestige is involved. However, I cannot picture a group of parents sitting around watching their toddlers play, and one parent saying to another, "I hope Suzy grows up to be a doctor or a salesperson."

Like any profession where people can make a lot of money, salespeople are highly scrutinized. What do you picture in your mind's eye when you picture a used car salesperson? Typically, you are not going to have a great visual (unless you are married to, the parent of, or are one). However, many outstanding individuals go to great lengths selling pre-owned cars to drivers all over the world.

Salespeople can and do affect the success of their business every day. A salesperson must add value to the company every hour, day, week, month, or year—or else they will simply be adding costs. Although the same can be said for the salesperson's coworkers, their value-added effort may be easier to account for since they are visible in their attendance in the office or the plant. Unlike their coworkers, a sales representative's value will be statistically measured and quantified by each sales report and commission check.

The analogies that I like to use for a salesperson are the quarterback for the football (American) team, if you are a sports fan, and the conductor of the orchestra, if you are musician. Without question, these positions are the leaders of their respective "teams." Focusing on the football analogy, the quarterback could have the best arm, intelligence, and athletic ability in the league. But if the quarterback has receivers running the wrong routes and linemen who cannot block, the team's success is doomed. Teamwork is essential for success.

As a leader of the team, the quarterback is responsible for making sure there is communication and execution once the players are on the field. In the football analogy, you know that successful coaches (executive leaders) give their players the credit for the wins. The coaches are quick to accept the responsibilities for the losses. Throughout a football season, the coach who is having success will utter some cliché like, "I haven't won a single game this year since I haven't been between the lines when the clock was running." So, who leads the team when the clock is running? The quarterback (salesperson). This control and field leadership is why the quarterback is usually the highest-paid player on the team, much like salespeople. It is why, when things are not going well, fans, media, and sometimes the teammates target the quarterback for the team's lack of success. It is true for the salesperson as well.

Stories from the Road – #3

Real-world Lesson: Going the "extra mile" will gain respect and referrals.

Since those who sell previously owned cars (also know as used car salespersons) are people too, I wanted to share an example of one car salesperson whose service impressed me. My mother and father live in a small rural community in Ohio, and they lived on a fixed income in their retirement years. Like me, Dad knows where the key and the gas holes are and that is about it.

They needed a used late-model minivan, and their friends recommended Joe, a man who sold used cars. If you gave him the specifications of the vehicle you wanted, he would find the perfect vehicle for you. Joe traveled to auto auctions and talked to people about their trade-ins for months for Mom and Dad. He would drop by unannounced with a vehicle for them to try out. If they were not home, he would leave it at their house so they could test-drive it. Later, he would return to pick it up and get their feedback. He provided a tremendous service to my parents. They finally settled on a trade-in that had low miles at a great price. My parents were more than satisfied customers and regularly referred him to their friends.

When I was going through sales training for a manufacturing company, I began to realize how important the salesperson is as a team leader. I was required to work on the shop floor for three weeks before I went into my sales territory. It made me a better salesperson by working directly with our products, and I was amazed to find the interest level of many of the plant workers in my future sales. To their credit, they wanted to know everything about my territory, my major accounts, and whom I would be prospecting. They wanted me to be successful since it would mean job security for them. The other thing this experience did for me was to make me want to "work for them" by picking up the phone and making that extra call when my motivation was not at its highest level. It gave me great satisfaction that my efforts not only helped keep those workers employed, but those same projects helped them hit their production bonuses, which resulted in additional income for them.

Prestige and ego may be factors associated with going into sales, but one has to understand the ramifications of the leadership role within a company. All industries are different in terms of how they view the sales representatives, but rest assured that companies highly value the sales representative role. Prestige does not mean famous, and you won't be signing any autographs as a salesperson. As with any high-profile and well-paid profession, the "bad apples" who exploit the freedoms of the sales position create stereotypes that the rest of the salespeople have to live with.

Valuable Business Experience?

The idea of being in sales to gain business experience is not a new idea. As mentioned earlier, there are no positions closer to running a business than sales. Salespeople are the first line of offense and defense for a company. Market information developed through conversations with customers and prospects is the lifeblood of how the business is directed. It is how products are developed, priced, and marketed. Consequently, salespeople have a good understanding of the business challenges and opportunities. It is also why many companies spend (or should spend) so much of their training budget on their salespeople.

Experience is also why a lot of salespeople take jobs with companies or industries that might provide skills to get to their next position or business opportunity. It is no different than the restaurant entrepreneur who works at McDonald's to learn the best practices for restaurant efficiencies, challenges, and opportunities before starting his or her own restaurant.

Stories from the Road – #4

Real-world Lesson: Take jobs that will help you grow as a salesperson.

I had two offers when I graduated from college. One job offer was from a lesser-known sporting goods manufacturer in my very own territory. I would cover five states in the Southwest, and my compensation would include a car allowance, salary, and bonus. In that role, I would work from an apartment in Dallas, which was 1,000 miles away from my home in Ohio and 700 miles away from my sales manager in Tennessee.

The offer that I accepted was from a well-known sporting goods manufacturer with a long history and fantastic brand recognition. I accepted a sales trainee position for $20,000 less than the salary of the other offer! Additionally, I did not receive a car allowance or a bonus plan. My rationale for accepting that position was that I wanted the experience of working in a global headquarters and being in a formal sales training program.

I never regretted that decision because it made me a better *outside sales representative* in the end. I learned from and worked with about forty outside salespeople as well as the consumers of the sporting goods equipment in that role. A few sales reps taught me how NOT to treat your inside support. I learned to always go the "extra yard" to take care of my *inside salespeople* after that experience of being on the other side. The year I spent in customer service as a sales trainee in an underpaid, understaffed, and underappreciated role made me recognize and understand the commitment it would take to succeed in *outside sales*.

In conclusion, there are many reasons why people look to sales as a career. Money, lifestyle, prestige, and experience are some of the unique drivers. But to whom much is given, much is expected. Hard work, persistence, and organizational skills are what keep people in and excelling at their sales jobs.

SECTION II – WHAT SALES JOB IS FOR YOU?

CHAPTER 2 – EVALUATE THE INDUSTRY

"When you come to a fork in the road, take it."

– Yogi Berra

Hall of Fame Catcher, New York Yankees

What Type of Sales Positions Are There?

Although Yogi Berra intended his remark for visitors coming to his house, it has become a favorite quote for commencement speeches across the country (including my own). The quote is to encourage new graduates to embrace uncertainty and the life decisions that they will face. The same is true for people who have an interest in sales.

All companies place a high value on talented salespeople. Since quality salespeople are in high demand, they will encounter "forks" (read: opportunity) as they progress through their careers. All career decisions have risks! It is my belief that the wise salesperson evaluating a new opportunity benefits from an orderly evaluation of the industry, the company, and the position itself before accepting any offers. It is much more rewarding to work in an industry and for a company that is expanding rather than contracting because of job security and income potential.

Job Evaluation Process

2.1

INDUSTRY

then

COMPANY

then

POSITION

Stories from the Road – #5

Real-world Lesson: Start with the big picture in mind when evaluating your career planning.

When you are first trying to get into sales, the first offer might be your best offer. The thing to remember and focus on when starting out is where you want to end up. The jobs you accept create your "brand" and are a part of your education.

Personally, my most important experience of reviewing the industry, company, and the position before making a move came at a time when I was evaluating five offers. I had the opportunity to do a FULL job analysis after the software company I was selling for melted down during the dot-com bust. In short, I won the "Salesperson of the Quarter" award, and I was "let go" the next quarter to reduce costs and position the company for sale. I was confident in my ability to find a job even though the economy was reeling. My wife was five months pregnant with our first child, which added pressure.

It is rare that a successful salesperson gets to interview with enough companies to receive five offers at the same time, but I made the most of my "extra" time to interview. It became my full-time job. I considered each opportunity using the evaluation criteria in this chapter, and I accepted the job that best suited my long-range goals. Money was a factor, but again, it was not the most important thing to me because I recognized that I wanted the experience associated with the job that I accepted.

The "Job Evaluation Process" may seem obvious, but many people move right to the career search Web sites and job postings on campus for the current job openings regardless of industry. They start submitting resumes without the proper due diligence. If they are lucky enough to get an interview, they read up on the company so they aren't caught off guard by the standard interview question: "Why do you want to work at ABC Corporation?" Is this scenario familiar?

If you start by researching the industry first, you can answer the questions by telling interviewers why you like the industry, the company, AND the position. They will be impressed with your research and interest. If you do not do your research, and you are lucky enough to be hired; you could end up in an industry that you don't like or that might provide limited personal growth. To further compound a wrong career decision, it can be very challenging to move from some industries, creating prolonged professional delay and increased job dissatisfaction.

The Industry Evaluation

What do I mean by industry evaluation? You must understand the particular challenges and opportunities of the industry you will be selling to before you accept any position. The days of picking a "good" company without evaluating the industry are long gone. That does not mean you cannot get lucky, but it is highly unlikely that you will achieve maximum satisfaction and job security. This industry evaluation is part of your high-level and long-term strategy. It builds your contingency plans if things unexpectedly deviate from what you desired with your first company or position. If that happens, you have the industry experience to fall back on to find another company or maybe just another sales job with the same company because of your industry background and knowledge.

As illustrated in figure 2.2, these factors make up the industry segmentation. Although General Electric (GE) is technically one company, it is really a conglomerate of many companies called business units with each

General Electric's Business Units

2.2

GE COMMERCIAL FINANCE
(Business Unit)
- Capital Solutions (Business)
- Corporate Financial Services
- Healthcare Financial Services
- Insurance
- Real Estate

GE INFRASTRUCTURE
- Aviation
- Aviation Financial Services
- Energy
- Energy Financial Services
- Oil & Gas
- Rail
- Water

GE HEALTHCARE
- Diagnostic Imaging
- Global Services
- Clinical Systems
- Life Sciences
  - Medical Diagnostics
  - Integrated IT Solutions
  - Interventional, Cardiology and Surgery

GE MONEY
- Credit Cards
- Retail Sales Finance Programs
- Home Loans
- Personal Loans
- Motor Loans & Leases
- Corporate Cards
- Credit Insurance

GE INDUSTRIAL
- Advanced Materials
- Consumer & Industrial
- Equipment Services
- GE Fanuc Automation
- Inspection Technologies
- Plastics
- Security
- Sensing

NBC UNIVERSAL
- Network
- Film
- Television Stations
- Entertainment Cable
- Television Production
- Sports/Olympic Games
- Theme Parks

Source: www.ge.com, 2007

one operating in its own industry. If you interview for a sales position with a business unit of GE, you must first research that specific industry. The fact that the company is GE really does not matter until you are satisfied with the industry. The company analysis of GE is step number two in the three-step process.

Would You Prefer Selling a Product or Service?

If you do a career search online, one of the search filters is "industry." When you click the drop-down box, you will see a long of list of industries. What now? The way I evaluate industries is by what they sell. Do they sell a product or a service? Is it tangible or intangible? Are they business-to-business (B2B) products or services? Are they business-to-consumer (B2C) products or services? Do you have a preference about what you would like to sell?

The Industry Segmentation Matrix, Figure 2.3, further expands the concept of how the products and services of GE would differ greatly from a selling perspective. It is worth noting that even within GE's business units the businesses can fall into different quadrants.

Stories from the Road – #6

Real-world Lesson: Sell what you like to sell.

A close friend of mine left the software sales field after several years to get his real estate license and pursue a career in real estate sales. He said he could not stand selling software anymore. It was a conceptual sale with long and drawn-out *sales cycle* and a very low frequency of success unrelated to his efforts. With no pun intended, his comment to me was that it was good to finally sell something that was "real."

All sales positions are different, and it is almost more important to know what you do not want as it is to know what you do want. The great thing about sales is that every industry needs salespeople. Pursue one that is interesting to you. If you don't like it, learn as much as you can to sharpen your selling skills and move on to another industry or company since many of those skills do transfer.

GE's Industry Segmentation by Business Unit

2.3

	SERVICE	PRODUCT
TANGIBLE	**GE COMMERCIAL FINANCE** ▮ Real Estate **GE INDUSTRIAL** ▮ Equipment Services	**GE INFRASTRUCTURE** ▮ Aviation **GE HEALTHCARE** ▮ Medical Imaging
INTANGIBLE	**NBC UNIVERSAL** ▮ Film	**GE MONEY** ▮ Credit Cards

27

There is no right answer to what is better to sell. It is more of a personal preference among salespeople since there are pros and cons to selling services and products.

The Pros and Cons of Selling Products and Services

2.4

	SELLING PROS	SELLING CONS
PRODUCTS	▌ Physically defined product ▌ Hot products means **money** for Salespeople	▌ Sales success is tied to the company's product innovation ▌ Shipping coordination ▌ Returned/expired goods ▌ Product availability/ manufacturing lead times ▌ Buyers are price focused
SERVICE (Intangible Products)	▌ No shipping or freight issues ▌ Typically higher commissions and bonuses ▌ Happy customers rarely change ▌ Salespeople are critical to sales success	▌ Longer sales cycles ▌ Personnel issues can cause quality problems ▌ Differentiation is hard to demonstrate

Growth or Mature Industries?

You can evaluate an industry life cycle just like a *product life cycle*. It looks like a bell curve. There are five phases: early growth, growth, mature, decline, and in some cases an end, as illustrated in Figure 2.5.

Industry Life Cycle of Video Recording Devices

2.5

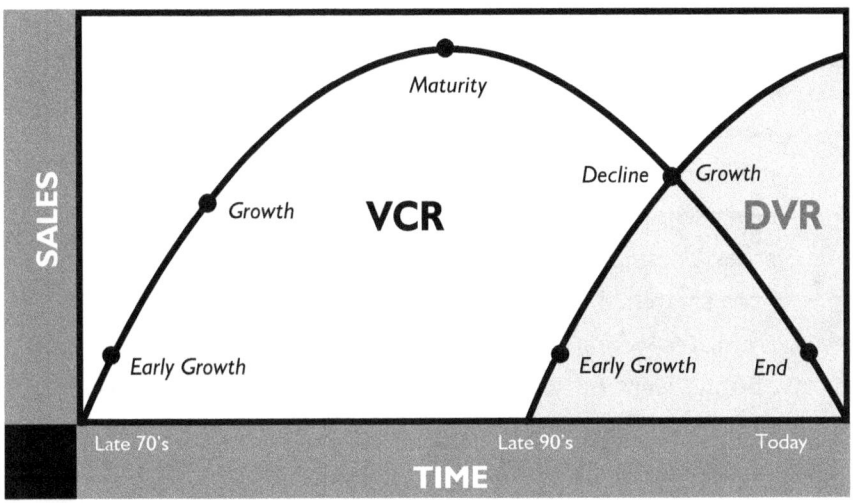

The bell shape nature of the industry life cycle comes in a variety of shapes. The shape depends on the time to complete the full cycle and the length of time for the phases. Examples of two very different shapes would be gasoline-powered automobiles and VHS tapes. The gasoline-powered automobile is very mature and moving toward the "assisted living" state at the age of one hundred plus years with alternative fuel vehicles gaining acceptance. The VHS industry is all but dead at the ripe old age of "twenty something" with the adoption of DVDs and digital recorders becoming mainstream.

There are challenges on both ends of the life cycle spectrum for salespeople. Salespeople selling new products can spend a lot time educating clients and getting "the door slam" until the "early adopters" of new technologies appear. Early adopters are people who can be described as change facilitators since it is their early decision to buy that allows business ideas to grow in popularity without having to rely on history.

> ## Stories from the Road – #7
>
> **Real-world Lesson: Understand the *sales cycle* and *product life cycle*.**
>
> In 1998, I went to work for a venture capital-backed software company. The experience was fantastic even though it ended with a fiery crash with the dot-com bust. I have never worked for a company like it; everyone pushed each other because of a commitment to build the company from scratch. The stock options that were granted to each employee were great motivators as well. Essentially, stock options were only going to be worth something if the company went public or was sold at a high value because of its success.
>
> That aside, we were building cutting-edge software that was revolutionary at the time. Our *business model* was delivering our Customer Relationship Management (CRM) software via the Web. I know it doesn't seem very revolutionary now with the leading CRM vendors all delivering their products in that manner. At the time, we were calling on company CIOs who had never heard of Web-delivered software, let alone seen it demonstrated.
>
> From a sales perspective, it was a case of good and bad news. We were able to offer a revolutionary product but, on the downside, we had to find the early adopters who were willing to take risks on our new technology. The bad news from a sales perspective is that early adopters are hard to identify when prospecting. It was always

easy to find prospects who wanted to see the demo, but 95 percent of the time, we were providing a free education on the latest technology because they thought it was "bleeding-edge" instead of leading-edge technology.

On the mature to declining side, products and services tend to have declining profit margins and low client loyalty because of the variety of buying options (commoditization). In this environment, the best salespeople gravitate to the low-cost-producing company so they can still be competitive with price and make sales commissions. Often, it becomes more difficult each year to make the same or more money in a declining market.

There are two opportunities for a salesperson to reap short-term windfall sales in a declining market.

- Competitors failing: If competitors leave the sector or merge with others, the remaining companies have the opportunity to accelerate their sales efforts to gain market share and sales.
- Sales peers leaving the company: It is the "vulture sales" concept. If a salesperson leaves the organization, the other salespeople circle around the sales manager. They can sometimes "swoop" in and harvest the fruits of the departing salesperson's pipelines.

No matter what, salespeople should recognize the writing on the wall and should start to look for other industries to move to as soon as possible. Those blips of encouragement last only so long, and it makes for a difficult work environment because of the cost cutting and merger activity.

Examples of appropriate questions you should ask:

- What changes are you seeing in your industry?
- What are the greatest sales challenges in your industry?

- Is the industry growing or shrinking?
- What are the opportunities for growth?
- What do you like the most about your industry?

Industry Culture

Culture in the business world can be described as the personalities, work ethic, and physical work environment. Like companies, industries have their own unique cultures and selling environments. The construction industry varies drastically from the insurance industry, which is altogether different from the software industry for salespeople. It is all personal preference, background, and attributes of the salespeople that will make one comfortable with a particular industry. Therefore, it is good to understand the industry culture before getting into it.

With every industry, salespeople have a different value. This is what I will call "sales value." What do I mean by this? It is simply the way salespeople influence sales with their knowledge, relationships, negotiation skills, or time investment in the sales process.

In some industries, the sales value of the sales role tends to be quite high. In most cases, that sales value transfers directly into their compensation. Figure 2.6 illustrates how sales roles have different sales values to an organization depending on the uniqueness of a product and how much a buyer relies on the knowledge and assistance of the salesperson.

Salespeople with relationship-building skills, specialized educational background, or technical certification are adding value by using their experience and knowledge. The law of *supply and demand* tells us this because these people are hard to find and costly to replace because of their unique qualities.

Sales Value vs. Compensation

2.6

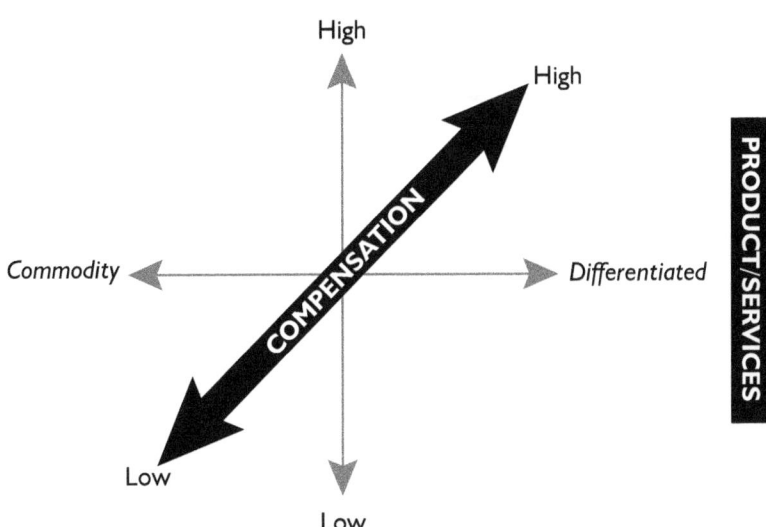

VALUE ADDED SALES KNOWLEDGE

High

High

Commodity

Differentiated

COMPENSATION

Low

Low

PRODUCT/SERVICES

Stories from the Road – #8

Real-world Lesson: Industries value salespeople differently.

The industry culture shock was enormous when I went to work for the start-up software company after spending five years with a twenty-five-year-old construction products company. The "eye-opener" for me was that there was very little loyalty shown to a software salesperson by the company. That was completely different than the construction products industry.

Why was this lack of loyalty the norm? The biggest reason for this attitude in the software industry is that there is a ZERO value placed on relationship-building skills. Salespeople are paid to sell the software and move on to the next deal. Unlike many other industries, software salespeople are paid to be "*hunters*" and not "*farmers*" since once the deal is won or lost, they move on to find the next deal.

Many of the salespeople and sales managers at the start-up had backgrounds with large software companies. Their stories about former coworkers who landed large six- and seven-figure deals one month only to be let go the next quarter were shocking to me. Not all software companies are that way, but it is definitely the industry culture as a whole.

Having spent time in other industries, I recognize this management by "fear of losing your job" as very short-term thinking. I tried to remove that pressure to sell from affecting my conversations with my prospects. "Fear" will and can cause salespeople to do and say things to prospects that will cause more harm than good to the company sales and image. Other industries recognize the value of salespeople and the investment they make in the training, relationships building, and the *sales pipeline* development. They recognize that sales turnover has a high cost, and firing salespeople is a last measure.

Industry culture is important to consider since you might find a company that you like but it is anomaly in the industry. What happens if you get frustrated with your current company? You run the risk of having sales skills in an industry you no longer want to work in because you do not respect your current competitors enough to work for them.

How do you evaluate industry culture when interviewing? The best resources for career research and job opportunities tend to be in your network of contacts. Parents of your friends and classmates can be your best leads and advice. Educators also provide valuable insight if they are familiar with you and your personality. By leveraging your resources, you can identify people in the industry you might be targeting to get an unbiased perspective on that industry's culture.

If you are already interviewing, ask the people who are interviewing you about their perspective on the industry. Cross-reference that with their opinion about the company's culture that you observe. Why are they similar or different? Ask to meet with an *outside sales representative* to interview him or her about the job if you have met only with management. Better yet, see if it is possible to observe firsthand by asking to do a "ride along" day with an *outside salesperson* or a two-week internship with no pay. These investments of your time will give you invaluable experience.

Additionally, a good indicator of how an industry and a company value their salespeople is to evaluate the "turnover rate." A high turnover rate indicates a low value for the salespeople or at least low job satisfaction. You will want to compare turnover at the company you are interviewing with versus the industry average to get an understanding of what kind of job security and stress you can expect.

In summary, when you start your analysis and research at the industry level, you will have the appropriate background to make informed decisions by asking the right questions during your final decision about the position that you are interviewing for with a certain company. From your research, you might determine that it is the wrong industry, which will prevent a bad decision. Or you might like the industry, but you conclude that you are interviewing with the wrong company in that industry. In any case, researching the industry is a step that you should not overlook.

CHAPTER 3 – EVALUATE THE COMPANY

"People are definitely a company's greatest asset. It doesn't make any difference whether the product is cars or cosmetics. A company is only as good as the people it keeps."

– Mary Kay Ash

Founder, Mary Kay Cosmetics

People? It is all about people at the company and not how smart she is. Mary Kay Ash is the CEO of America's leading cosmetics company. Like many successful entrepreneurs, she recognizes that the early risk taking and ideas might have stemmed from her vision and how she launched the company. However, there are many great ideas that end up in the garbage in the form of a business plan. It takes people committed to an idea and vision to breed and grow a successful business. Or, as one successful business owner that I worked for liked to say, "The banks have all the money. All I have is people."

Although it was published in 1996, Bill Gates' book *The Road Ahead* was filled with business wisdom and foresight. It is particularly interesting reviewing it now to see how his observations back then are coming true: "Information Appliances," "The Content Revolution," "Friction Free Capitalism," and "The Internet Gold Rush." These predictions were right on the mark considering eBay and Amazon were just hiring their first employees and the dot-com rush was years away. However, it was the "richest man in the world's" comments about how companies spiral that will stick with me the most:

> "When you have a hot product, investors pay attention to you and are willing to put their money into your company. Smart kids think, hey, everybody's talking about this company. I'd like to work there. When one smart person comes into a company, pretty soon another does because talented people like to work with each other. This creates a sense of excitement. Potential partners and customers pay more attention, and the spiral continues, making the next success easier.

> Of course, companies can get caught in a negative spiral too. A company in a positive spiral has an air of destiny. One in a negative spiral operates in an atmosphere of doom. If a company starts to lose market share or

delivers a bad product, the talk turns to, "Why do you work there?"

Once you have selected the industry you want to pursue, picking the company becomes the next challenge. Along with the people at a company, there are other factors to consider when you are evaluating companies. The biggest points that you will consider and assess are the quality of the products and/or services of that company, the company's ability to deliver on their offerings, the size of the company, as well as the resources available to you to accomplish your selling goals. Additionally, we will review how a company's training, advancement opportunities, financial strength, culture, and testing also become a part of the analysis.

Public vs. Private (Big vs. Little)

Go "BIG" early in your career if possible! One of the biggest questions is whether to pursue the large public companies or look for a smaller privately held company when you initially start your search. Experience with a large company early in a career is a great background to have for a variety of reasons, all of which fall under the "experience" and "resume building" categories.

For small companies, it is difficult to offer what a big company offers to a new salesperson such as: formal training, career advancement path, and talented senior managers to educate and mentor "new" salespeople. There is a lot more "independent learning" at a small company since formal training programs are expensive to provide and maintain from a company perspective. In fact, this is why small companies try to recruit talented salespeople with "big company" experience so they don't have to make that investment in formal training for their newly hired salespeople.

Early in my own career, my coworkers and the large corporate environment provided the best business and career education. Those coworkers and managers were some of the most important relationships in my sales development. My sales peers were "in the trenches" with me because of their accessibility and experience, and they provided some of the best insight when I was in a sales rut or I needed tactical or strategic help with my sales efforts and development.

Another benefit in starting with a large company is the professional network that you build. Your peers will provide you with future job opportunities as you and they move into various roles at your company as well as positions with other companies. It is like the old adage about *"It is not what you know, it is who you know . . ."* (My favorite asterisk to that saying is those who know you have to like you and respect your talents enough to recommend you). In addition to having a large sales force, your sales peers at a large company usually (not always) will have a better professional network, educational background, and job experience than those sales peers at a small company.

So, why would you work for a small company first? It can be a personal preference. Things like culture, the work experience offered, the financial opportunity, and personal reasons (like not wanting to relocate) are all reasons why someone might start with a small company first. Furthermore, it might be your only offer, and you need the sales experience (and the rent is due). In any case, we will compare the following items that will come into play when deciding on a big or small company.

Pressure

The ownership of the organization can drastically affect the sales philosophy and pressure applied to the salespeople. Publicly held companies have an ever-increasing responsibility to "hit" the projections for earning that they provide to Wall Street on a quarterly basis. Investors have even slammed public companies' stock prices even when they have exceeded their revenue projections. That is why there is much greater pressure on salespeople to forecast sales and deliver on those projections than ever before.

If the pressure to hit the numbers for Wall Street were not enough, the Sarbanes-Oxley Act, signed into law on July 30, 2002, and effective as of August 2003, holds officers of the company legally responsible for forecasts and actual financial statements. Introduced in the wake of several corporate financial scandals such as Enron and WorldCom, it protects investors by holding the company executives personally responsible for financial forecasts and disclosures. Company executives have had to revise and improve the process and frequency by which they gather and report their financial information.

The "everything flows down hill" theory applies as far as the pressure on salespeople at public companies. Since it is the CEO and the CFO whose necks are on the line, the executive team pressures the sales managers to give accurate and increasingly detailed sales projections. That pressure flows down to the salespeople from the sales management in the form of *sales quotas*.

There have already been instances since the introduction of Sarbanes-Oxley where sales managers and salespeople have had to provide signed forecasts as to provide a "paper trail" in case anyone challenges the executives on the numbers they have provided. The worst part of this effort is that forecasting and re-forecasting consumes a great deal of sales managers' and salespeople's time, and it adds no value for the clients.

Private companies on the other hand can vary greatly in regard to "pressure." Some try to mimic the look and feel of a publicly traded company with an emphasis on making the quarterly quotas, while others are more informal with their approach toward quotas and forecasting. Most privately held companies look only at the yearly number to determine the success of a salesperson. Many business owners argue that this approach is better for achieving long-term business success versus a short-term quarterly focus that will result in a more "natural" close and reduce the price discounting of those deals.

The best compensation model will make the best salespeople apply their own self-induced pressure to sell more and make more money for them and the company. Quotas and forecasting add a considerable amount of cost because of the *opportunity costs* associated with managing them. Whether you sell for a public or a private company, the one constant is that the sales numbers speak for themselves, and salespeople dislike forecasting. The extra *sales quota* pressure that salespeople experience can vary greatly between public and private companies.

Just Sales or Is There More to it?

The Small Business Association (www.sba.gov) states that 50.1% of the private (non-government) workforce is employed by the 22.9 million small businesses in the USA (2002). The public companies and large private companies tend to have more than 500 people but represent only 00.3% of all businesses. The excitement for many talented salespeople working for small to mid-sized private companies is the fact that they have to do more than just sell. They are very important with strategic direction in areas such as marketing, brand development, recruiting, collections, inventory forecasting, and product development.

Large organizations are fully equipped with staff to support these salespeople in all sectors of the business. Therefore, smaller organizations' salespeople get to wear all of these hats on a daily basis. Some salespeople like the challenge of the full involvement in the small business environment while others view these duties as distractions from their mission of selling. Therefore, the size of an organization can be a factor in expanding your job "function" from your job "description." It is worth recognizing and understanding what type of company and sales role appeals to you now and in the future.

Training

Sometimes, the last thing that salespeople consider or ask about when interviewing is the training that they will receive. Most people ask how they will be trained for the job they are being hired for, but they do not consider a company's ongoing commitment to training.

As mentioned earlier, large companies are better suited for providing formal and structured training. The corporate training staff is expected to be aggressive and to come up with creative and necessary training to keep the employees up to date on the latest professional trends, cross training, and technological advancements. The commitment to training ensures that people are available for advancement in the organization and makes the salespeople effective in their daily functions.

Additionally, the large companies are typically much better with formal performance reviews. In the reviews, there is always a section dedicated to training. The trainers and sales managers are responsible for creating and tracking company-based training. Sales managers want to avoid problems with the HR department due to lack of compliance for subordinates' training so they tend to make sure their salespeople get the required training.

Because of costs, small and midsized companies rarely have an in-house staff. Training needs are outsourced to a third party training center. Budget requests for training are sometimes the last approved item in the discretionary budget. So, in most cases, the training at large companies far exceeds the training that small to midsized companies offer. Again, the training is a reason that small companies look for employees among people with large-company experience.

Appropriate questions to ask about training:

- What training can I expect?
- How is the training focused: product training, selling skills, the company's software systems, and personal development?
- Do you train in-house or do you outsource it to a third party?

"Advancement"

Advancement in sales, like beauty, is in the eye of the beholder. One person's concept of advancement might be moving to a sales manager position while another person's concept might be to start his or her own company. At a large company, successful salespeople, typically, see a variety of career opportunities much faster than they would at most smaller companies.

Promotion opportunities create their own issues at large companies. There are many political implications when positions are offered to employees or when employees request to interview for positions that are posted at the company. When a new position is offered, there is usually an "invisible" corporate pressure to accept the offer. This stems from the idea that you will be passed over in the future as other opportunities come up if you say no too many times.

Likewise, large companies provide "advancement temptation," which can cause stress between you and your manager if you put your name in repeatedly for open positions. Some managers do not like to see their direct reports leaving at all because it causes more work for them finding, hiring, and training a new hire. In addition, they will be challenged in hitting their *sales quotas* (translation: their bonus) with sales representative turnover.

"Begin with the end goal in mind" when you are interviewing and accepting a new position. This is the most important advice I can give to someone wanting to enter into the sales profession. I compare accepting any position as the place where you pound the stake in the ground and start your journey to the next stake. If you are in New York, do you really want to drive through Florida to get to Chicago? You can, but why do it? What is your next job after the one you are interviewing for? How will the job you are interviewing for help you get there quicker?

Sales Experience

3.1

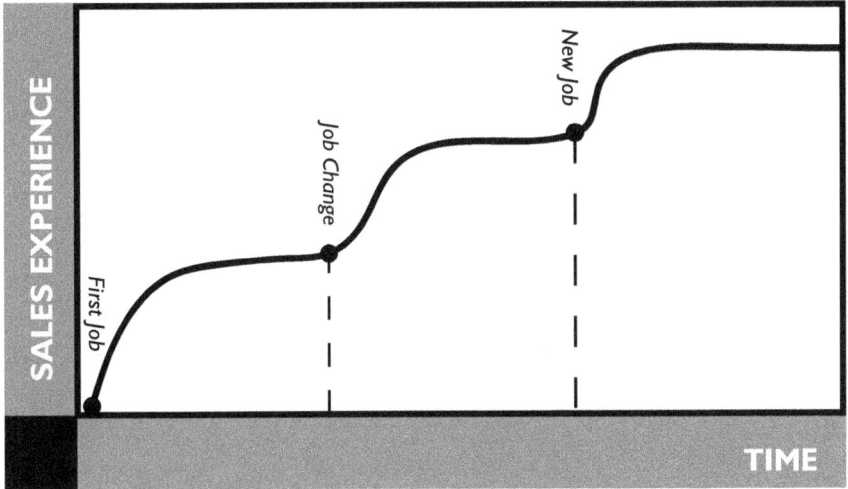

Financial Strength

A company's financial strength is important. This might seem obvious to most people, but many organizations are not profitable on a consistent basis. Many "start-ups" have not made a profit in a quarter, let alone a year. Many of these same companies employ a large number of salespeople.

Obviously, it is easy to research public companies profitability. The Internet is loaded with online search tools. Yahoo! Finance is one good resource that is free and easily accessible for public companies. Private companies are harder to research, but some reporting agencies still provide detailed information about their credit worthiness. D&B (www.dnb.com) and OneSource (www.onesource.com) are a couple of leading providers of credit and business information on privately held companies. You can pay anywhere from $10 to $150 per report depending on the level of reporting you want. This could be a cheap investment compared to making a bad company choice.

It should be no surprise that at a profit-challenged company, the salespeople end up doing many things for themselves, because the additional support staff and budget are not there.

Stories from the Road – #9

Real-world Lesson: Signs you should reevaluate your company and industry.

All companies and industries go through challenging economic times. In addition to those challenges, managers and financial people move into new roles in organizations all the time. The people are trying to make "their mark" for their company, and they are sometimes in a position where they need to save a company from going out of business. Aside from dire financial emergencies, you can count on a few ridiculous requests from your company to save money.

My favorite requests are:

- "Please try not to use your cell phones, and shorten the length of your calls. Try to use pay phones."

It was 1993 when a mobile phone bill could be $350 per month, but the efficiencies more than made up for the costs.

- "Please do not use the color printer since the cartridges cost more than the black and white cartridges."

You know your business is in financial trouble when your CFO sends an e-mail like this.

- "We are not participating in trade shows this year."

I think it was a reaction by management after calculating how much they spent on trade shows the previous year. Actually, we ended up doing MORE trade shows that year since they were a critical marketing opportunity for our industry.

These requests are financially noble, but not well thought out. We are SALESPEOPLE! I was waiting for the company to request that we charge our clients and prospects mileage for OUR sales calls.

It will be up to you to decide how to react when you get requests like these, and you will. In most cases, they are just a reaction to recent revelations about a certain cost. It should not be a sign to start looking for another company and industry without more information on what is really going on at the company.

Profitable companies do not recklessly throw around money but they are not under same pressure to reduce costs as unprofitable ones. From a sales perspective, your company's business viability is one of the biggest concerns of your prospects and customers. Aside from a *RIF* at an unprofitable company that directly affects you, your company's credit worthiness can create a sense of hesitancy by the buyers and hamper your sales. Therefore, it is worth the extra effort and expense to do the research on your target companies to understand what challenges might lay ahead with regard to its financial strength. Ask yourself, would I invest money in this company? If not, why invest your career?

Who Is the Management and What Are Their Philosophies?

The management of the organization creates the culture, sets the business vision, and attracts the quality of the employees. More importantly, they are also responsible for the organization's success or failure. Therefore, it is important for you to determine your list of criteria that will reveal if a company's management philosophies and personalities are right for you and your future career goals.

Successful companies tend to mix entrepreneurship with a disciplined process that allows high-caliber people to perform at their maximum potential. Therefore, try to gain an understanding of company operations through formal and informal channels. Does the company's management have an entrepreneurial focus and business agility? Or are they political and cumbersome by nature?

That said, focusing only on the manager to whom you will directly report is a common error and is not a good strategy. What happens when that person is promoted or leaves the organization? What then? What is the caliber of talent available in the organization to replace your manager?

If, during the interview process as an *outside salesperson*, you do not meet people higher in the organization than your future sales manager, you should not accept an offer. They should respect your request to interview with someone at least one level higher than your future manager. If is a privately held company, I would always ask to interview with the owner(s). Most owners will take a sincere interest in people hired into sales positions with their companies since they recognize that salespeople are the "face" and the "brand" of the organization.

The typical information that I like to find out through the interview process with the management team includes:

- Educational backgrounds
- Professional experience

- Industry-specific experience
- Management tenure with the company
- Management philosophies, style, and beliefs
- Evidence of personal and professional integrity

There is no question that you must evaluate your future manager. You must respect that person for his or her background, management style, business philosophies, and experience. If you do not think highly of your manager, you will face long days and frustration. Additionally, your boss will play a large role in how successful you will be since he or she will determine your accounts, your leads, and your training schedule. However, it is important to look to the next level up in the corporate structure to better understand the company's philosophies that will determine the company's overall success.

Stories from the Road – #10

Real-world Lesson: Make lemons into lemonade when working for a boss you do not care for.

After my promotion to a larger territory, it was no secret that a sales manager I was going to report to was going to be difficult to work for. I knew that the salesperson I was replacing requested his transfer to another territory. The salesperson I replaced said my new boss was very meticulous and demanding. It did not take me long to understand that his description was accurate.

He was the type of sales manager who on Monday morning wanted a "write-up" of every sales call I made the week prior. After he reviewed the one- or two-page "write-ups," he would invite me into his office to ask me a bunch of follow-up questions about what I turned in. He was like a professor who never stopped asking questions about papers I turned in instead of just giving me a grade. I thought he had this paranoid illusion that his bosses in New York expected him to know everything about my accounts. He also made the comment to me one time that it was his job to get the most out of me to protect the stockholders' interest. At that moment, I knew that was a quote that I had to remember to understand what our relationship was. I was his means to an end to drive sales for his territory.

He was organized to the point of obsession. He once had a meeting to discuss how we should conduct our meetings. He thought they ran too long, and he was not getting the right kind of market intelligence and feedback from them.

If you add on that I had a "salary only" compensation plan, it was a miserable situation from a job satisfaction perspective. However, as a second-year salesperson, it was the best training I could have had at the time. He improved my writing skills, sales skills, and my future managerial skills since he always focused on making me a better salesperson, leveraging his twenty plus years of sales experience and sales management.

It is important to analyze the manager you will be reporting to, but it is important to analyze how good a teacher that manager will be and what you will learn in your role. You should have the confidence and belief that you will enjoy learning from the managers and the management style of the company. It will also increase your possibility for happiness and, consequently, success for you at the company.

Company Culture

Have you ever said or thought, "This company just feels right (or wrong) to me"? What you are thinking about is the company's culture. It is comprised of the intangibles such as the people you meet during the interview process combined with the physical surroundings of the office. A company's culture is very important to understand and recognize during the interview process since you will have to be associated with it every day you work there. It culminates as an emotional sense or "feel."

If you are interviewing in a field sales office, try to arrange a trip to the headquarters to interview. This is not always possible in an entry-level sales position, but as your sales career advances, it will become more important. The best feel for the company culture will always be at the headquarters. A regional manager may mask some of the culture at the local office, which may be a good or bad thing from your perspective.

Every company has a culture. Some companies try to overtly create and display their cultures while it is more subtle at others. Culture is something to consider when you are evaluating a place of employment since your association with it is a reflection of you. Conversely, the interviewing company will try to analyze whether you will fit into its culture for the same reason.

Stories from the Road – #11

Real-world Lesson: The signs of culture.

Maybe it is because I have been on thousands of "sales calls" evaluating each company's culture. Those signs have become second nature to me. If you ask any experienced sales professional about it, he or she will tell you what to look for in evaluating a company's culture.

The clues that help identify the company's culture are as follows:

- Does the company have a written description of its culture on its Web site?
- What part of town is the business located? Downtown? Suburbs?
- Condition of the exterior and landscaping of the building?
- What kind of cars are in the parking lot?
- Décor of the lobby? Updated?
- Reading materials in the lobby? The Bible? *Wall Street Journal*? *Sports Illustrated*?
- How are people dressed and groomed?
- Are the desks in the office tidy or messy?

An example of one company that prides itself on its culture is the great company of Cintas. Its culture is something that Cintas prominently addresses and considers a point of differentiation in its literature for prospective employees. All office staff and salespeople are in formal business attire everyday. EVERYONE in the headquarters wears a name tag. Cintas also requires employees to keep tidy offices with very few personal items displayed on their desks. Cintas' culture is very different from today's "business casual" standards, but the company's unique culture contributes to its repeated ranking as one of "America's Most Admired Companies" by *FORTUNE* magazine.

For the record, the majority of companies today are "business casual." However, they still prefer or require formal dress for their salespeople at least on initial meetings with prospects or customers. In some instances, however, the prospect or customer insists that the salespeople dress "business casual" during the appointment-setting process.

Standardized Testing at Companies

When it comes down to making the "best choice" of companies to interview with, it becomes your personal preference. Since there are no perfect companies, salespeople look for a company or a division within a company that might be a "best fit" for them. Similarly, companies spend millions of dollars a year to test candidates to see if the interviewee would be a "fit" for his or her role in the organization's business vision and culture.

From both a company perspective and a job seeker perspective, the standardized testing tools are usually a last step that companies use to understand the candidate's likelihood of success. If a candidate is a good fit and is hired, the testing results can be very useful in managing the new employee. The testing summary report will describe the employee's personality, and then describe how to manage a person with those characteristics to motivate and keep his or her job satisfaction as high as possible.

Lastly, there is always the issue when presented with the personality profile section of the test to answer as you think the company wants you to answer. Honesty is still the best policy. Do not try to guess the "correct" answers. It will not do you or the hiring company any good to have false data, and therefore, the hiring will draw false conclusions about your personality.

Stories from the Road – #12

Real-world Lesson: Applicant testing can provide a lot of insight for the interviewee as well.

Yes, people do change. I twice interviewed with the same large publicly traded company separated by a twelve-year span. I really wanted to work for this company when I first left college because it was a great company that provided a fantastic sales training program for recent college graduates.

In my first attempt, the interviewing process was very successful for me. After an interview on my university campus, I went to a regional office and met with the district manager. The interview with him went well also. The HR department contacted me next to schedule taking their standardized personality profile as the last step to receiving an offer. A few days after the test, it was determined that I "did not pass" the personality profile. The district manager liked me so much he lobbied for me to take the test again! I learned from discussions with the HR people that this was unheard of. After I "failed" the test again, I did not get a job offer. It caught me way off guard because I thought testing was just a means to baseline my personality and a mere formality.

Twelve years later, a different manager at the same company pursued me with my years of sales experience under my belt. The interview process was again a success. I was amazed that they still wanted me to take the same test after my years of sales experience and the number of interviews that I had this time. However, the results were different this time, and they said my score was "excellent." They shared with me that I scored really well in the categories that were very important traits for their salespeople to possess. Ironically, I was the one who turned them down this time since I had a better offer from another firm.

"Passing" the test the second time revolved around my sales experience, which had made me more challenging and skeptical (versus too trusting and naive). In fact, a few years after not passing the test the first time, I was required to take a personality profile test for a different company that I worked for at that time. The test results indicated that I was off the charts in the "trust" category. After that testing was combined with a couple of situations in which my trusting nature was violated, I made a conscious effort to change that personality trait to be more skeptical and to challenge what was said or done in the business setting as well as my personal life.

In the end, the company is a very important factor in how happy you are on a day-to-day basis because of your interaction with your peers, management team, and the company culture. The next chapter will provide more insight into how the position itself plays a factor in your development.

CHAPTER 4 – EVALUATE THE POSITION

"If you work just for money, you'll never make it, but if you love what you're doing and you always put the customer first, success will be yours."

– Ray Kroc

Founder of McDonald's Corporation

Sales, as Mr. Kroc said, is all about the customers. It is understanding how they think, their current needs, and what they want (sometimes before they know they want it) to keep them happy and loyal. There are many different types of buyers. All of them won't be customers and all of them won't be friends, but it is in your own best interest to treat them that way.

As one senior purchasing agent emphasized at a lunch early in my career, buyers are people too! He shared with me a story about how a salesperson with whom he worked with for many years introduced him to one of his acquaintances as one of his "customers." That introduction broke down years of friendship that the buyer felt he had built up with that salesperson. He was giving me interesting and very beneficial advice. From that point on, I introduced everyone as my "friend." It is not an insincere gesture because that is how I view 99 percent of my customers.

When analyzing sales positions, there are many intangible and tangible factors to consider. This chapter is dedicated to those points that will require your considerable review and analysis. Before we can analyze those items, we must understand what type of sales positions are available for you to pursue. In a 2007 paper entitled "A Typology of Sales" by Dr. David W. Rosenthal of the Farmer School of Business at Miami University (Ohio), Dr. Rosenthal categorized all sales positions into seven broad categories:

1. Business to Consumer (B2C)
2. Missionary (aka – Detailing or Specifying)
3. Channel I
4. Channel II
5. Professional/Semi-technical
6. Technically Enhanced
7. Strategic Capital Goods/Service

Each of the seven sales categories requires some unique selling skills. My conclusion is that about eighty percent of the selling skills are the "base" selling skills that are very transferable between categories and other sales positions. The remaining 20 percent is what is unique to that position and category. It is, also, that 20 percent that will cause someone to like or not like a particular position or category.

In Figure 4.1, the table provides further detail on each of the sales categories.

What Will You Learn in Your Job?

Sales positions vary as much as salespeople. It is best to fully understand the responsibility of the sales position being offered before accepting. When comparing sales positions, one of the first and most important things to analyze is what will you learn in your sales position. This experience is what you will carry with you for future jobs and is a valuable part of your compensation.

For instance, the next company will be more interested in what you did and learned in your prior job(s) than what your income was. Yes, the compensation you earned at your prior company is important because it becomes a benchmark for negotiating with a prospective new employer. However, your historical sales results as well as the industry experience, industry contacts, and competitive insight you have will greatly influence your future compensation.

From Whom Will You Learn?

As mentioned in the previous chapter, the people with whom you will work with on a daily basis are big factors in this learning experience. You will want to analyze your manager for how he or she will aid in your development as your mentor. In addition, you should not forget to evaluate your peers.

Your peers are your brothers and sisters "in the trenches." They are pivotal informal sales trainers. Prior to joining an organization, it is always my recommendation to meet with as many salespeople as possible. You will

Sales Types at a Glance

4.1

CATEGORY	DEFINED	CORPORATE EXAMPLES	# OF CLIENTS	COLD CALLING	SALES SERVICING	COMPEN-SATION	OVERNIGHT TRAVEL
B2C Direct (Excluding Retail)	Selling direct to the end consumers and individuals	Insurance, Real Estate, Financial Services, Mortgage Lenders	Many	Heavy to begin Less later	Little to begin More later	Draw, Commission	Very little
Missionary	Calling on decision making "influencers" to make recommendations of your product or services to the buying party	Brand Pharmaceutical Sales (i.e. - Pfizer), Engineered Products Sales (i.e. - Johnson Controls)	Many	Heavy to begin Less later	Average sales servicing involvement	Salary + bonus	Limited
Channel Sales I	Selling your products or services to accounts that then resells the products to the consumers.	P&G, Coca-Cola Enterprises, PepsiCo, Enterprise Rent-A-Car	Limited	Limited	Heavy Involvement	Salary + bonus	Limited
Channel Sales II	Channel sales that requires training of the retailers or distribution staff to sell the products or services being offered.	Shaw Carpet, Black & Decker, Gallo Wines, John Deere	Limited	Limited	Heavy Involvement	Salary + bonus	Limited
Professional Semi-Technical	Selling products or services into organizations that will use those items for building their own products or services.	Cintas, Ashland Chemical, Xerox, MeadWestvaco, Intel	Varies	Heavy to begin Less later	Little to begin More later	Salary, Salary + bonus, Commission	Medium to Heavy
Technically Enhanced	Remote selling via phone or web conferencing	Total Quality Logistics, C.H. Robinson, CDW	Many	Heavy to begin Less later	Little to begin More later	Salary, Salary + bonus, Commission	Very little
Strategic Capital Goods	Complex products and services that require a sizable investment and will alter the way the organization conducts its business.	GE Aircraft Engines, Deloitte & Touche, Grant Thorton, Leo Burnett Worldwide, Caterpillar, SAP, Oracle	Few	Limited - Accounts are known	Little hand off to team	Salary, Salary + bonus, Commission	Periodic

Source: 2007 paper entitled "A Typology of Sales", Dr. David W. Rosenthal of the Farmer School of Business at Miami University (Ohio) used by permission.

learn and socialize in and out of the office from these people. Many companies make this a step in their interview process. If they do not offer you the opportunity to meet some salespeople, you should definitely ask to interview with them prior to accepting any offers. Better than asking for an interview is asking for a ride along day when they are making sales, so you can really get a sense for the position as well.

Examples of appropriate questions to ask sales peers to gain insight about the company's philosophies are as follows:

- How long have you been working for the company?
- What are successful salespeople at this company especially good at doing?
- How does this company "value" salespeople?
- Help me understand how I report my activity to the sales manager.
- How often do salespeople have formal meetings and training?
- How would you describe your sales style and how that relates to the philosophy of the sales manager?
- How would you describe the *sales cycle*?
- How do you quote prices?
- How are proposals and orders processed?
- What is the salesperson's involvement in the quoting process?
- How would you describe the buyers you call on?

Who Will Your Sales Manager Be?

Sales managers are usually salespeople who achieved sales success and have many contacts in the industry. Seek to understand the sales manager's perspective. Some can make the jump to sales manager look easy; but for others the switch from a "doer" to a "motivator" is a difficult transition for many salespeople.

Why is this important to you? You should be aware that if your future sales manager is new to his or her position, it could take a few years to get adjusted and to create a management philosophy. I know that was the case for me in my first sales manager's position. It is not unusual for a new sales manager to take years to find the proper balance to get results through others. If you will be reporting to an experienced sales manager, that person will have a distinct management philosophy that I am sure will come out during the interview process.

To complicate sales managers' roles, some companies require the sales manager to carry a direct *sales quota* in addition to the management responsibilities. This is the organization's effort to save overhead costs and put the best talent on the best accounts. From a salesperson's perspective, the good news with this trend of multitasking sales managers is that they are in tune with real market conditions. However, the bad news is that your development time is sacrificed. Therefore, it is best to evaluate and understand your sales manager's perspective and experience as a sales manager to appreciate what to expect when you report to him or her.

Examples of appropriate questions to ask sales managers are:

- How long have you been a sales manager?
- How would you describe your management style and philosophy?
- Help me understand how I should report my activity to you.
- How often do we have sales meetings?
- Do you still have direct sales responsibilities?
- What are successful salespeople at this company especially good at doing?
- How much do the top, middle, and bottom salespersons make?
- How would you describe the *sales cycle*?
- What selling software do you use to manage the sales efforts?
- How are leads distributed to the salespeople?

What Selling Skills Will You Learn?

What is the company's commitment to training salespeople? Large companies will have this question down pat since they have formal programs in most cases. A sales manager for a small or a mid-sized company will tend to shift in the chair a little when asked this question since very few have a formal plan for training.

Stories from the Road – #13

Real-world Lesson: Big companies tend to have better training programs and embrace sales training.

Company training programs vary greatly. The second company I went to work for was a Fortune 500 paper company called Westvaco (now MeadWestvaco). At the time, its Management Trainee Program (MTP) was recognized as the leader in the paper industry. In fact, it was so renowned that headhunters would call and leave voicemails for management trainees during and shortly after completing the MTP. Westvaco dedicated the first four months to sales and management training in their headquarters in NYC. The training included selling skills, industry-specific training, and negotiating skills.

In my first role as a sales manager, the small company I worked for had no formal sales program. We had a small sales force of nine. I trained my sales team by leveraging the selling methodology that I learned at Westvaco, customized for our particular products.

My view on sales-specific training is the analogy about stopping to sharpen the saw if you are a lumberjack. By stopping to sharpen the saw, the lumberjack will cut more wood. I introduce this to convey that you should embrace sales training. Be a sponge! I am always amazed when senior salespeople reach the point when they think sales training is a waste of time. My feeling is there is always something more to learn, and it provides a reenergizing effect on someone who might have fallen into a selling rut.

In addition to the basic product training, some companies will actually adopt a sales methodology for their salespeople. Two examples of widely accepted selling methodologies include Miller Heiman (www.millerheiman.com) and Solution Selling (www.mikebosworth .com). If you know that a company has a preferred methodology, it would help if you could discuss the basics of the methodology by researching in advance of interviewing. Even if you know the methodology, it might be good to ask the interviewer about his or her interpretation of it to see how ingrained it is in the organization or if the interviewer has customized it into his or her own methodology.

In addition to understanding the sales training, make sure you understand the sales skills required for the job. Different sales positions require many sales skills. For instance, if you are in *specification sales*, you will not learn the art of negotiating pricing for a contract, but you should learn about building strong relationships with the people you call on. Some salespeople seldom give presentations to large groups while others give presentations to larger groups only. Salespeople who sell commodities tend to deal one on one with a purchasing agent. "Creative" salespeople (advertising or architect) tend to deal more with a group sales setting.

As a new salesperson, you will need to know in advance the training that you will receive (if any) and understand the "on-the-job" sales skills that you will need to succeed.

These are examples of appropriate questions to ask about training and specific selling skills that you need:

- Is there a formal sales training process?
- Is there a preferred sales methodology that is followed?
- What sales-specific skills will I need to have?
- Negotiating training?
- Public speaking?
- Proposal writing?
- Customer Relationship Management/Sales Force Automation software training?

Stories from the Road – #14

Real-world Lesson: Sales skills vary greatly from one position to another.

The most popular example of *specification sales* is that of brand pharmaceutical salespeople. Their goal is to educate and answer questions for doctors. They leave product samples for the doctors to use at their discretion. Their position dictates that they don't (literally) get a signature on a contract, a *PO#*, and leave. They will ask that the doctors support them by writing prescriptions for the pharmaceuticals they are specifying, and their sales efforts are then tracked by what are called "Zip Code" reports. The reports detail the prescription volume and measure increases (or decreases) in their area by the doctor's DEA (Drug Enforcement Agency) number.

Even though they are in the same industry, salespeople for a generic pharmaceutical manufacturer have a completely different role. They do not call on doctors. Their products are commodities by their definition.

Commodity salespeople tend to compete on price, quality, service, availability, and relationships (corporate and personal). They are calling on skilled contract negotiators who tend to focus more on price than anything since the product quality is assumed since it has to be FDA (Food and Drug Administration) approved. Therefore, the generic salesperson role tends to be one of a negotiator instead of a presenter of benefits and features to influence future decisions by the doctors.

What Industry-specific Skills Will You Need to Learn?

All sales jobs will have some "special" skills that you will need to learn if you are new to that industry. Some might be technical in nature and very necessary for sales success while others might be from an efficiency perspective.

Here is a short list of "special" skills examples that are helpful to have in advance of selling a product or service:

- Metal/Plastic Fabrication Sales – CAD (Computer Aided Design) plans reading skills
- Mortgage Broker – Financial calculations and spreadsheet skills
- Pharmaceutical Sales – Biology and chemistry classes
- Software sales – Computers, networking and databases

Some of the technical skills relate to the educational requirements in the job description, but often they are not requirements. Often, salespeople will be hired without these technical skills and the company will train them formally and informally. The pharmaceutical industry, historically, has not always hired salespeople who have a science background. However, they have very extensive training programs to educate their salespeople about the products they are selling.

Stories from the Road – #15

Real-world Lesson: Industry-specific skills should not be overlooked.

I remember when I completed my training for a plastic piping company in the fabrication shop. I got my first set of engineering drawings for a **RFQ** (Request for Quotation) that was to go out the following week. My sales manager handed me the CAD drawings for a large project at a chemical plant that used intricate fabrication. He then said for me to do the "take off." My first thought was, *What the heck is a take off?* Which was quickly followed by *How do you do it?*

My job was to estimate how many feet of pipe, fittings, valves, and piping fabrication we needed. Needless to say, it took me about 24 hours to do it and double-check my work. It was a six-figure quote that I ended up winning. The same project six months later would have taken me about a half a day after I learned this special skill of doing a take off.

In most cases, the only way to understand what "special" skills you will need for any sales position is to do a ride along with a salesperson or to work in the industry as an intern.

What Will You Learn about "Business" in General?

We have established that the variety of sales positions is enormous. Included in that vast chasm is the degree to which companies require their salespeople to focus on selling only. On the contrary, other companies, typically smaller companies, need salespeople to be "utility players."

They are asked to provide critical business feedback, direction, and strategy because of their proximity to the marketplace. Their business and industry understanding becomes critical to marketing, finance, and product initiatives. Those salespeople in "utility roles" are learning more about general business than just selling.

Additionally, I have always enjoyed participating in the tactical and strategic direction of the company while other salespeople would choose to stick to only selling. The opportunity to participate in strategy sessions will facilitate cross-functional training by working with marketing, finance, and other parts of the company's management teams. The size of the company dictates this informal training. The smaller the company is, the greater the need and ease of including salespeople in strategic planning. Therefore, it is not a coincidence that I have really enjoyed working for smaller companies during my career where my input and efforts had a direct impact on the corporate strategy.

Your Role in the Organization vs. Your Title

4.2

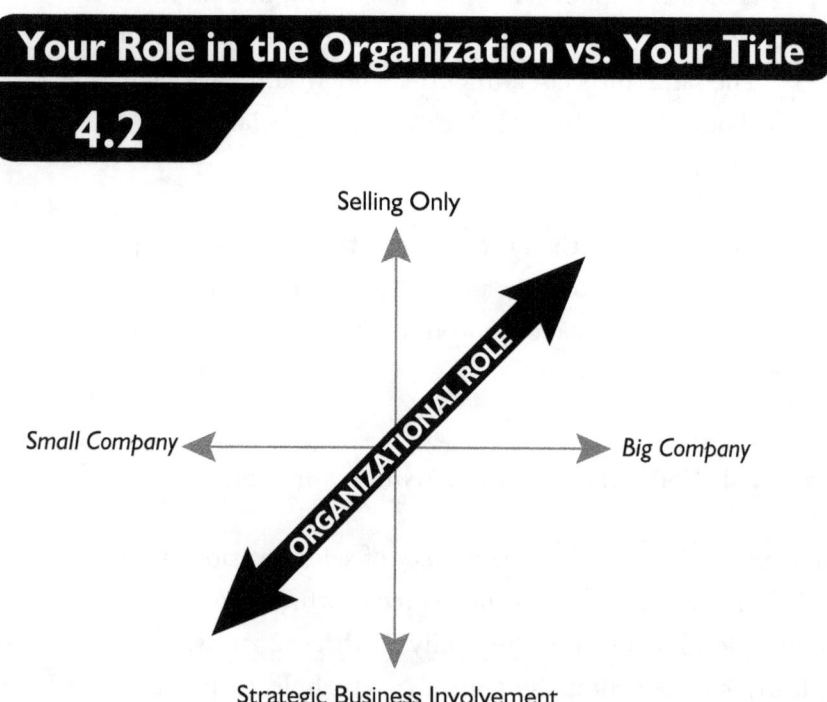

Ask yourself these questions to help you assess the business skills that you will learn:

- What transferable business skills will I learn?
- What involvement will I have in the marketing decisions?
- Will I work closely with the finance team?
- How will I utilize my writing skills?
- How much influence will I have on the overall business vision and strategy?

To Whom Will You Sell?

Will you "call on" CEOs or laundry managers? Does it matter to you? I know, I know, all the sales performance books you read tell you to call on the executive level first. Is it the CEO of a $50 million manufacturing company or one with five employees? It might be good to call on someone in as high a position in the organization that makes sense when you are cold calling. Depending on your product or service and the size of the company, you usually end up dealing with other appointed people in the organization with that decision-making capability anyway.

To illustrate this point, consider a contract with one company that might be worth $100,000. That is a lot of money by anyone's standards. If the contract were for bed sheets to a hospital chain, the CEO's assistant would more than likely direct you to the contract manager or the laundry manager. Why? The bed sheets are a commodity and not a strategic business decision, and the dollar volume does not warrant the CEO's input.

The opposite spectrum would be if you were selling $5,000-$20,000 copiers to small businesses. In most instances, you will have to meet and present to the CEO or owners of the businesses to get the signature on that contract because it represents a substantial investment to the small business. Although the dollar amount is smaller, you are selling to the CEO/owner who has a different personality and sales cycle than a laundry manager.

> ## Stories from the Road – #16
>
> **Real-world Lesson: The people you sell to and their physical location for sales calls can be an important part of your job satisfaction.**
>
> A great example of how people are different is how two people can view the same sales position. My "Tale of Two Brothers" best illustrates this.
>
> Dean and his younger brother, Davis, were working for a large and successful textile company in the same position but in different geographical territories. The job required extensive car travel since the territories were large geographically. They, like most of the company's salespeople, were salespeople earning over $100,000.
>
> Their customers were large hospital chains, long-term care facilities, and buying groups that needed their bed sheets, pillowcases, and curtains. The people they called on day to day to get feedback on their products were the laundry managers.
>
> Dean absolutely loved his job and the people on whom he called. They tended to be older women with whom he spent endless time earning their trust and becoming friends. He and his wife often visited them together, showed them pictures of vacations, and baked them cookies; in turn, these laundry managers reciprocated.

Davis, who is still a successful salesperson today, did not like the job at all and left the company. He disliked the fact that he was calling on people to whom he did not relate that well, and his sales calls often occurred in the hot and humid "bowels" (basement) of the facilities where the washers and dryers were.

It was an example of two brothers with two very different perspectives of the same job.

Therefore, when you are interviewing for a sales position, you should consider whom you would be calling on from a job satisfaction perspective. The company that is interviewing you should make this compatibility a top priority for its evaluation of you. Companies typically formally or informally profile their customers to get an understanding of what type of salesperson would work best with their customers and prospects. The best way for a salesperson to get an understanding of the people to call on is to do a day in the field with a salesperson to meet some customers and get a better understanding of who their contacts would be on a daily basis.

What Is the Opportunity for "Advancement"?

"Advancement" is in quotes for a reason. It is human nature to want to advance in a company and organization. When most people think "advancement," they think of doing something other than what they have been doing and adding responsibility. For salespeople, advancement can mean many different things.

There are salespeople who will get "burned out" of sales. For burned out salespeople, advancement can mean doing anything other than sales. Often, people who have sales success are the first to get promoted into sales management since members of management want their sales efforts to be replicated. However, seasoned salespeople often consider the sales manager position a demotion. They have been around long enough to know that a sales manager's role will require more work. Mentoring and managing multiple salespeople along with reporting to management or owners will create a loss of scheduling flexibility and independence. In addition, it requires a different skill set to manage people, budgets, and forecasts instead of sell.

The crux becomes that sales managers often make less money than their best performing salespeople since they are now viewed as overhead. A very blunt comment by a mentor of mine alluded to this when I was talking about my promotion to my first sales manager's position at my company with him. His comment was, "That will be good experience for you, but why do you want to make less money?" Humm... Work more hours, travel more, deal with personnel issues, and make less money. His words were ringing in my ears after my first review as the sales manager since I knew what the top salespeople were making. Many sales managers end up going back into sales because they are successful at it, they can make more money, and they prefer the lifestyle.

Another form of "advancement" might be starting your own business. With a large majority of business owners being former salespeople, it is not a leap for salespeople to get the "entrepreneurial bug" to start their own business. As mentioned earlier, the best salespeople think as if they are running their own business. They do some simple math to determine how much they earned and how much the company made from their efforts. For those who enjoy taking on risk, they will "advance" into owning their own company.

What Kind of Sales Support Can You Expect?

Sales support can vary greatly within the same company. Any sales support role is to aid in the efficiency and success of salespeople. Therefore, pay close attention to the following areas when interviewing for a sales position:

- *Inside sales* support
- Technical sales support
- Administrative assistance

These support positions are important to analyze in advance so you can set your expectations. For instance, one company (or one division within a company) could provide a full-time assistant while others provide no administrative assistance.

Appropriate questions about sales support:

- What administrative assistance will the company provide?
- Do I work with a specific *inside sales* or customer service person? Can we meet?
- How does the company handle technical sales support?

Marketing Strategy

It would be important to know the company's marketing strategy and the products you are selling. Is the company launching TV advertisements? Or is hiring you the company's marketing and advertising strategy and budget? Marketing is important for the salespeople because it can be a source for leads and builds a brand that opens doors for salespeople. Therefore, you should make it a point to get an understanding of the company's marketing strategy.

Appropriate questions about the marketing strategy:

- What does this year's marketing strategy consist of? Radio advertisements? Print advertisements?
- Is the marketing strategy expected to provide leads for the salespeople?

Leads vs. *Cold Calling?*

Lead generation is always a contentious issue for salespeople. Salespeople always want more. Leads can be a function of the company buying expensive lists with the company names, key contacts, and important company information. Or, they could be as simple as you and the "Yellow Pages." Therefore, you should not overlook this detail since this can dramatically affect your efficiencies and income depending on the type of compensation package you have.

What Is Your Office Setup?

This question is not: How comfortable are the office chairs? It is, simply, for you to consider the logistics of the office or lack of one in the case of a salesperson working out of his or her home.

As mentioned earlier (Stories from the Road – #4), I rejected the first sales job offer largely because I had to work out of my home and not gain the experience from working with other salespeople. After three years of sales success, I accepted another position in which I worked out of my home.

Unique Brand or Is It a Commodity?

What is the gap for differentiation of the product or service you will be selling compared to your competition? It will be very important to be satisfied with the type of product positioning you will be selling. Is it positioned as a luxury item with no equal or is it a commodity that can be sold in a reverse auction for the lowest price? This can have a drastic effect on how you conduct your day-to-day activities and consequently affect your job satisfaction.

This can best evaluated by a brand-to-commodity spectrum. A well-branded product has many unique features and benefits that cannot be replicated because of patent protection or superior brand loyalty. Additionally, new

Brand vs. Commodity Spectrum

4.3

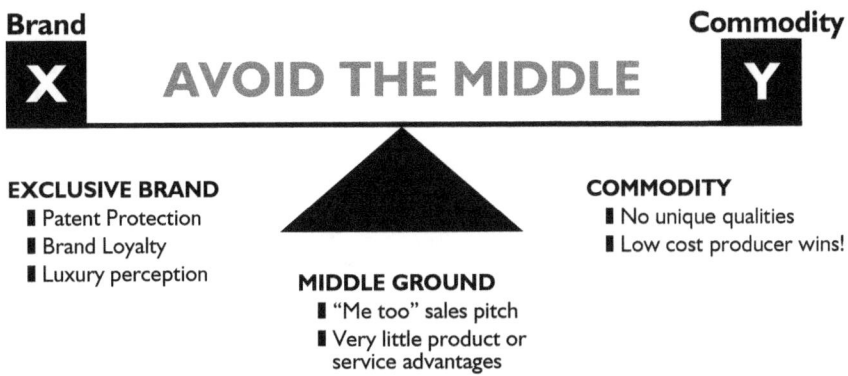

Brand

Commodity

| X | AVOID THE MIDDLE | Y |

EXCLUSIVE BRAND
- Patent Protection
- Brand Loyalty
- Luxury perception

MIDDLE GROUND
- "Me too" sales pitch
- Very little product or service advantages

COMMODITY
- No unique qualities
- Low cost producer wins!

products or brands have to create their own market by teaching buyers a new way to do things or explaining why their product is different.

On the opposite end of the scale, a commodity product has many "me too" competitors that make profitability a challenge. The low-cost-producing company is the winner at the lowest-priced commodities sale. It is worth mentioning that if the product you are selling is "stuck" somewhere in the middle, that is bad thing for the salesperson's commissions and the company. It becomes very difficult to explain why you are the best buying choice for disciplined procurement people.

In summary, there are many tangible and intangible factors in reviewing potential sales positions. The items covered in this chapter will help you understand your sales role and the challenges in that role. These points will ultimately help determine your potential job satisfaction and professional growth.

SECTION III – ANALYZING SALES JOB OFFERS

CHAPTER 5 – SALES COMPENSATION

"If money is your hope for independence, you will never have it. The only real security that a man will have in this world is a reserve of knowledge, experience, and ability."

– Henry Ford

Founder of Ford Motor Company

Why do people who have a lot of money often say things like "money isn't everything"? For them, their financial wealth sprang from passion, creativity, and the drive to be successful (or the fear of failure). However, passion doesn't pay the rent. Let's talk money and compensation packages.

Companies' use a variety of sales compensation plans to attract and keep their best sales talent. It can be very confusing for someone new to sales. Every industry and company has a different way to create an incentive for salespeople. It is important for you to be familiar with these terms when you are interviewing so you can converse intelligently regarding the pay structure the company is offering.

When job offers come your way, you will be in position to make tough decisions quickly. It might be your first offer or an offer to switch sales jobs. Whatever the situation may be, this chapter is dedicated to better prepare you for the pros and cons of those offers.

Stories from the Road – #17

Real-world Lesson: Your reaction and response time to job offers does matter.

I was offered and accepted one sales position that was a direct result of another person outside of our company not making a decision on a sales job offer quickly enough.

The owners of the company pulled the offer from a candidate because they interpreted his delayed decision as a lack of desire to work for them. He said he wanted to talk to his current boss to let him know his decision before committing to the offer. The owners' perception was that he was leveraging their offer for negotiating power with his current employer. If he asked for a day to come up with questions or to talk it over with his spouse, I think he would have been working for the firm.

Decision Factors for a Job Offer

5.1

PROS	CONS
▮ Experience the position would provide ▮ High income potential ▮ Good manager to mentor me ▮ Very little overnight travel ▮ Great industry	▮ Low salary ▮ Long commute to office ▮ Not the perfect company culture for me

When presented with an offer, you have to make a decision to accept or reject the job offer. For me, that decision-making process usually ends up with a blank piece of paper split with a large "T." One side will be a labeled "Pros" and the other side "Cons." Figure 5.1 provides an example of how you might lay out your analysis of an offer.

There can and should be many factors that will be listed as pros and cons. In most cases, the two most important items to consider for any sales position are money and experience. Although this chapter focuses on the very tangible aspect of income, the experience you will receive from the position is important and should directly tie in to your long-term goals.

In this chapter, we will explore the mystery that surrounds the various calculations for sales compensation models.

Experience Compensation

Understanding the value of experience versus money when you are beginning your career is very important. My first offers upon graduation from college made me quickly understand the concept and analysis that one must perform. The "money versus experience" decision I had was accepting a sales trainee job working in customer service with no commitment to when I would get a sales territory as opposed to another offer for a sales position that would immediately have a sales territory in the same industry. The job I accepted was $20,000 dollars less with no opportunity for commission.

Why did I accept the offer for less money and a lesser position? At twenty-one years of age, I wanted the experience of working out of a corporate headquarters with a formal sales training program versus working out of an apartment with very limited sales training since my manager would be 700 miles away. Many of my friends may have thought I was crazy. They may have thought the higher offer would be a perfect situation since I would be guaranteed great money, and I would have incredible independence working out of my apartment. I was honored by the offer and confidence this company had in my abilities to cover a very important territory for them, but I sacrificed the money ($20,000 in starting salary plus commissions) for the experience that I was seeking in my first professional job. Many years later, I am very glad I made that decision as that beginning organization did provide the building blocks of experience that I needed at that time for the future sales position I subsequently held.

Consequently, money is only one factor of compensation. One can argue that the experience of any job is more important in achieving your long-term goals and money aspirations. Sales positions are no different. Make sure you keep this in mind when you are choosing what industries, companies and positions you decide to pursue.

Financial Compensation Plans

There are many types of compensation packages crafted for salespeople. In this section, we will address and review the various sales compensation plans available. I will discuss the pros and cons of each from a salesperson's perspective.

1. Salaried Sales

Comment: You know what you will make.

A "salary only" salesperson is not a common arrangement, but for some industries and companies, it is more prevalent. In most cases, this set up will occur only at large companies where salespeople are responsible for such large sales volumes it is not possible to determine a commission plan that would be financially equitable for them and the company.

For salespeople who are "salary only," the challenge becomes staying motivated to prospect and deliver results. It is also why their sales managers constantly monitor and provide frequent "coaching" to these salespeople. If you were a sales manager, would you want someone who was "commission only" or "salary only"? Most sales managers want salespeople who are grinding to find the next deal because these salespeople want to make as much money as possible. Can salaried salespeople be grinders? Yes! However, people will tend to do what is required when there is not an additional financial incentive to do more. It is like paying a painter to paint your house by the hour versus a fixed fee. The fixed-fee painter will work as fast as he can while the hourly painter will take his time. It takes a special person to be an exceptional performer when he or she earns a salary only.

From the company's perspective, they can lose their best salespeople because of a salary compensation plan since aggressive salespeople don't have the capacity to earn above and beyond their salary. This problem can compound itself in that the same companies who are losing their best will also retain their worst salespeople. Their "high performers" tend to have a lot of confidence in their abilities, and consequently they have no problem switching companies for the right opportunity to make more money by delivering results. The worst performers don't want the risk associated with commission sales so they do not leave.

Stories from the Road – #18

Real-world Lesson: Salary sales can be a motivation and a money challenge for salespeople.

In my first *outside sales* position at a Fortune 500 company, I was twenty-four years old and responsible for a multimillion-dollar territory selling coated paper to large commercial printers in north Georgia and Alabama. Although the territory had a lot of responsibility, it was one of the smaller territories for that division of the company.

Our compensation plan was a straight salary with no bonus. I was happy doing what I was doing for the first year. I was learning a lot about sales by making a lot of sales calls, entertaining clients, and traveling all over the Southeast. After my first review with my sales manager, I realized that salaried sales was not an avenue to making money quickly by working hard. I expanded my territory by over twenty-two percent, and I got a five percent raise. My sales counterparts at the printing companies I was calling on were making up to four times what I was earning with their commission structure!

It was tough for me to want to work hard and schedule two or three weeks of travel in a month if I knew that I would make the same amount money. That is human nature. The job offers and the desire to get out of salaried sales were too great for me to stay with the company.

2. Salary + Bonus

Comment: Your income highs and lows are not extreme.

The salary plus bonus (S+B) plan is for those companies that have a large volume of sales like the "salary only" plan. The company offers a bonus to further focus the salespeople to grow (or at least maintain) the sales volume and objectives in their territory.

The typical S+B plan will have a sales goal established by the sales manager. Sometimes the sales rep will have some input on what the goal will be. Many times, they won't. The bonus will be achieved as a percentage of the established goals.

Sometimes the bonus will be tied to non sales-related activities. This is often referred to as management by objectives (MBO). This could include the number of new accounts established in a given time frame or managing the average days in which invoices are paid. The review and bonus often occur at the end of the quarter or year.

3. Salary + Commission

Comment: You have a "low water mark" with unlimited potential to make money. Warning: a high producer might sacrifice income by accepting the salary and a reduced commission rate.

The most common sales compensation structure is a salary plus commission. This allows a salesperson to understand the worst-case scenario in advance. A common saying is that the salary "pays the bills," and the commission equals "extra" revenue.

The base salary is negotiated according to experience level. A high base salary is usually reserved for senior salespeople who have the experience to justify it. More often than not in this compensation model, the salary tends to be on the low side for salespeople because there is a large up-side for results. The S+C model is often offered to those industries and companies that rely on the personal relationships and industry-specific knowledge that a salesperson has in selling the products.

Commissions are paid in two ways from a company's perspective. One way is to pay salespeople based on the "Top Line" number or gross sales number. You sell $1 million dollars worth of product or services, and they pay you five percent of sales. You make $50,000 in commissions. Alternatively, other companies pay commissions based on gross profit (Price – Costs = Gross Margin). You sell $1 million worth of product at a 20 percent gross profit. Gross profit of $200,000 multiplied by a commission rate of 25 percent makes the commission $50,000 as well. The commission rate will vary depending on the industry, the company, and the products or services being marketed.

Software, real estate, and insurance salespeople are good examples of pure "top line" or "gross sales" commissioned salespeople. In general, people selling services are usually paid commissions on gross sales while people selling products tend to be paid on gross profit since the calculation of costs is easy to define.

For many salespeople, salary and commissions are the best of both worlds for those who are risk averse. If the base salary is high enough to provide a good living, the commissions can provide additional discretionary income for investing and savings.

Stories from the Road – #19

Real-world Lesson: Make sure your sales commission plan is detailed in writing for all scenarios.

Companies have and do change the rules sometimes with commission plans once a large deal is won. I am familiar with many instances in which this has occurred. My best advice is to get commission plans in writing.

One particular example is when a sales representative at a payroll company won a multimillion dollar outsourcing deal with one of the largest companies in the world. The background was that he spent several years agreeing to lose accounts in his territory because he wanted to concentrate his efforts on this account. After he and his sales engineers finally won the business, his company failed to execute and deliver on the agreed-upon services of the contract. Over a six-month period, the company refused to pay the six-figure commission owed to him, and finally the contract was canceled; his company agreed to pay damages to the customer. He delivered on his responsibilities and made the sacrifices necessary to win, but his company did not deliver on its responsibilities.

Through the years, I have heard many disheartening stories about companies renegotiating or not paying commissions owed to salespeople because of the size of a large deal. Some of those instances ended up in a lawsuit brought by the salesperson (as in the case above) while many more ended up with the salesperson bowing to the pressure to keep his or her job by accepting the renegotiated commission.

This corporate failure to honor the financial commit-ments to the salespeople is a fact that you should be aware of, and it underscores the importance to understand and negotiate the compensation plan before you accept it (in writing).

3. Commission Only

Comment: You have higher risk, but equally you will have a higher reward if you produce.

If compensation drives behavior, then "commission only" salespeople focus on nothing but their customers and sales. What you sell is what you make. That is why this structure is the least desirable for people who are first starting out in sales. The fear of the unknown can be daunting. I know it was for me when I was coming out of college.

Why would a company offer a straight commission-only position? The four most frequent reasons for establishing a straight-commission com-pany sales force are:

Product: The *product line* of the company is not strong enough to sub-stantiate the cost of a full-time salesperson.

In the sporting goods industry, for instance, there are "rep groups" and *independent representatives* that sell on a commission-only basis for multiple companies. The sales representatives provide a valuable service by representing multiple *product lines* and/or companies thus reduc-ing the number of salespeople a buyer must "see." Additionally, many buyers rely on the input of their trusted salespeople for their buying decisions. The salespeople will provide market feedback on the hot products of that particular company and steer them away from the slow movers.

Industry: The industry can dictate what is considered the best way to sell the products and services.

Financial services products are often sold via commissioned agents. The insurance industry and stockbrokers typically sell on a commission-only basis because of their clients needs to buy multiple products, but they do not want to deal with multiple companies. These brokers provide the buying advice that best fits their clients' needs.

Money: Some companies do not want to invest the capital to support hiring, training, and managing full-time reps.

Start-up companies are forced to look at commissioned salespeople since they do not have the money to staff, train, and manage a sales force. Other disillusioned companies might not make their sales team a priority since they think their products and services sell themselves.

Speed: Companies may want to cross into new markets or geography quickly, leveraging *independent sales representatives* who already have relationships with the buyers they are trying to reach.

They recognize that the commissioned salespeople might sell their products bundled with other companies' products with more success since they already have important purchasing relationships.

Who would accept a position that pays commission only? Not many rookies could take on this challenge. For people just starting out, commission-only sales is very difficult because of the lack of training and guidance from the company and sales manager. It is not only difficult, it requires that you have money to get started to cover your start-up and selling expenses. Therefore, it would be difficult to recommend commission-only sales for a first job in sales unless there is a real passion for wanting the experience as a means to an end for the next job or it is your long-term career plan.

On the contrary, many proven salespeople that have the sales experience, confidence, training, and the bankroll of money necessary to allow for the additional risk will want to maximize their earnings as commissioned salespeople. Many senior salespeople may have a client base to forecast the amount of money that they will make, which will remove some of the risk of becoming a commission-only salesperson. Additionally, they like the independence and flexibility of working for themselves as a straight-commission representative and potentially carrying other companies' *product lines*.

As you can imagine, commission-only sales positions have commission structures that are much higher because of the additional risks associated with paying your own expenses and the lack of a consistent monthly salary. In short, you are running your own business.

4. The Draw Concept

Comment: You will have some security starting out with a base salary but you also have a financial "upside" opportunity if you achieve success quickly. But the financial security diminishes over time.

The draw concept is common when new salespeople with very little experience start with an organization. The company wants to protect itself from lazy salespeople whom they cannot monitor on a daily basis. The company is trying to attract quality people and protect the new salespeople from too much personal financial sacrifice if they are straight commission while they build up their *client lists*.

There are two types of draws. The "diminishing draw" is a higher salary to start, and it is replaced by commissions over time. In Figure 5.2, the diminishing draw" is a "step" draw where the salary is reduced over time. There is often a set time in which the salesperson must convert to straight commissions. Many plans give the salesperson a one-time op-

Optimal Conversion Point For A Draw

5.2

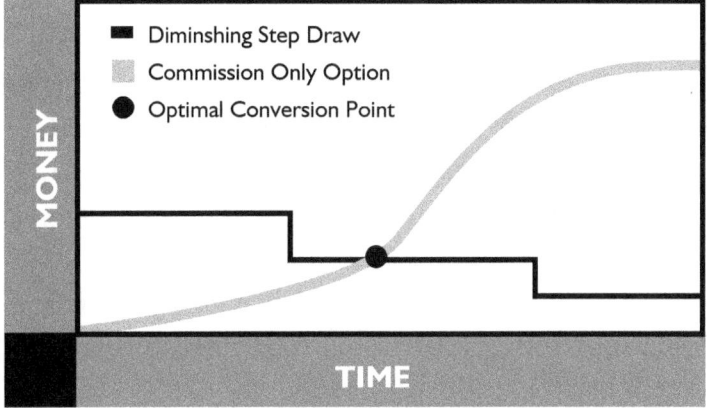

tion to convert to commission only at any time during the established draw period.

The other type of draw package is one that doesn't go away in time. This draw will tend to be a low salary that remains constant over time. It is intended to establish an earning floor for the salespeople and to cover living expenses. The idea is that the draw is subtracted from the commission earned on a monthly or quarterly basis. Therefore, it gives the benefits of both a salary and commission-only plan.

Many insurance and financial products companies have a draw plan for their new brokers or sales agents. An example would be the sales representative who receives a salary for a year. During that year, the salesperson would have enough time to build their "book of business" and move to a commission plan. If the sales representative achieves sales success prior to the year-end, he or she would have the ability to move off the draw and make more money on the commission schedule.

As a long-term strategy to keep salespeople from leaving after a bad quarter or two, some companies use the draw to establish a base salary, but the draw is deducted from the commissions at the end of a month or quarter. Recoverable and non-recoverable draw are the two types of draw plans. In either case, the draw becomes the lowest amount that the sales representative will make. The hope is that the sales representative will make a lot more than the draw from the commissions earned in the given pay period. If the commission calculation is less than the draw, the difference in the draw is applied to the next quarter for a recoverable draw plan. A non-recoverable draw plan would start anew in the next quarter with the negative balance from the previous quarter ignored.

In summary, sales compensation plans come in various designs. The plan that is best today for the company and the salesperson might not be the best one in the future. The company's products and services change (for better or worse) along with profit margins on those items. As salespeople gain experience and confidence, their professional outlook and personal priorities change. When interviewing, it is important to understand the financial compensation options and the pros and cons for you to make the most educated decision about which offer might be best for you.

CHAPTER 6 – LEGAL ISSUES WITH SALES POSITIONS

"Don't get it right, just get it written."

– James Thurber

American Humorist (1894–1961)

Disclaimer: Do not construe the following as legal advice; it is simply my opinions and points for the reader to continue to research and seek the appropriate legal counsel.

Like all trusting people, I have had my fair share of promises made to me that went unfulfilled. From his quote, it sounds like Mr. Thurber may have experienced some disappointments in the past as well. The need to put business details into a contract makes it such that salespeople need to be good amateur practitioners of business law since they are usually negotiating the commercial terms of the transactions. Depending on the industry, they may need to correspond with internal and external lawyers about the terms and conditions of a contract on a frequent basis.

In my years of sales, I have spent countless hours and learned much working with the various contracts and lawyers. As you can imagine, many customers want to put their stamp on contract templates. The customers might have different wants and needs that are not applicable in the contracts, or they might have objections to the wording that is included in those contract templates. Depending on your organization, those changes can be accepted or rejected. It comes down to the companies' contracting philosophies and the desire to appease customers or prospects to keep or win their business.

The three most important areas to understand and appreciate for new salespeople on a personal level are "non-compete clauses," "antitrust laws," and "professional liability." These three items represent your commitment to the company and external legal obligations.

Non-Compete Clauses

Sales positions vary as much as salespeople. You must fully understand the responsibility of the sales position a company is offering before accepting any offer. When comparing sales positions one of the first and most important things to analyze is what you will learn in your sales position. This experience is what you will carry with you for future jobs and is a valuable part of your compensation. That is why companies often ask salespeople to sign non-compete clauses.

If the non-compete is provided in advance, you should find a lawyer to review any non-compete clauses that you may need to sign. If it is not provided, you should ask if you can see any "employment agreements" that you will be asked to sign once you accept the offer. The laws around non-compete clauses vary from state to state, but the intent is the same. It is to keep you from starting your own competing business or working for a competitor in that particular market, leveraging the relationships that you have built from your time with that company.

The challenge arises when your personal lawyer "red lines" the document and you now have to think about how you want to approach the suggested changes with your employer (or not). Non-compete clauses can be challenging and emotional for the employee and the company depending on the details and lawyers' interpretations of the wording. The goal is to get through the discussion around any requested changes without lasting repercussions for either party. Since both parties are trying to protect their respective interests, there have been cases where parties could not work out their differences. However, most of the time the parties can find some middle ground on the requested changes.

Antitrust

As a salesperson who is negotiating pricing and business terms with customers, antitrust laws are a part of your daily job function. In 1890, the Sherman Antitrust Act made it illegal to form a monopoly or restrain trade. Congress passed it, in part, because of the railroads' efforts to monopolistically merge and raise prices. However, that same act is still in full force today. The U.S. Department of Justice still has ability to use federal court orders to stop illegal activity or impose remedies where appropriate.

You may scoff and think that antitrust laws deter only the decisions made in the boardrooms of the large companies of today but that is not the case. Salespeople are vulnerable too. It is worth reviewing activities associated with the sales process because, like all legal infractions, ignorance is not an excuse.

- Price Fixing – An agreement, written or understood, between competitors on pricing their products or services.
- Predatory Pricing – When pricing a product at a low price to drive competitors out of a market or prevent new competitors from entering a market
- Bid Rigging – Like price fixing, it is the practice of designating a winner of a bid before the bid occurs.
- Tying – The practice of making a sale of one good or service conditional on the purchase of second product or service.
- Vendor Lock-In – The cost of moving or switching becomes so great that it restrains customers from switching to a competitor.
- Geographic Allocation – It is the geographic agreement between competitors in which they decide who gets what area. Any requests for bids that are not in that company's territory are not bid or are bid at a high price.

Many large companies will often have their legal teams review these laws with their salespeople because they realize that they do not want to defend antitrust claims. When I worked for a Fortune 500 company, the corporate attorneys reviewed these laws with us and they discussed how to handle situations related to these matters. For example, they recommended we not talk to our competitors even if they approached us at trade shows so customers could not jump to conclusions about what we were discussing. If competitors approached us for any reason, the lawyers instructed us to say we could not talk to them and we were to report the activity back to the legal counsel. It seemed a little extreme, but we quickly understood that this was a serious matter.

Professional Liability

Since salespeople have an important role in representing their company's features and the benefits of their services and products, they can be held legally accountable for what they say and write in letters and e-mails. Although it is not common, there have been instances where false claims and/or faulty products or services have sent salespeople to the courtroom. It becomes a concern when the salesperson has acted as a "trusted advisor" with special training to support the sales effort.

Stories from the Road – #20

Real-world Lesson: Some salespeople have professional liability risk exposure.

You may have heard that anybody can sue anybody for any reason. However, if you are on the front lines of commercial transactions, you are a litigation target as a salesperson. One such case is particularly interesting to consider since the salesperson was sued under Connecticut's Product Liability Act (CPLA) as a pharmaceutical detail salesperson for a large pharmaceutical company (Oliva v. Bristol-Myers Squibb Co. D. Conn., No. 05-00486, 12/15/06).

In summary, the lawsuit was filed because Oliva (a consumer) argued that he had suffered severe injuries because he took pharmaceuticals his doctor prescribed for him that were manufactured by Bristol-Myers Squib (BMS). In the lawsuit, it also names the BMS salesperson who called on his prescribing doctor because he influenced his doctor to write the prescription while failing to provide adequate warnings to Oliva, health care providers, or the public regarding the inherent dangers and proper use of the medication.

This recent lawsuit is an illustration of how complex the selling process can be and how selling is defined. Although he was employed by BMS to market and detail the product, he "never sold, took, or processed orders" of the drug, played no role in its purchase by physicians or consumers, and did not finance any purchases. However, the courts found that he derived substantial economic benefit from his actions and he was to have extensive product knowledge and to have convinced the doctor to prescribe the medication to Oliva. This was enough for courts to find that he could be defined as the product seller, according to CPLA.

In summary, salespeople do have legal responsibilities. In addition to non-compete agreements that bind them contractually to their organization, salespeople should familiarize themselves with antitrust and professional liability regulations as they relate to their specific industries. If you have questions, it is worth asking the company you work for to meet with the legal team to discuss those items if they do not address it formally during your new employee training.

SECTION IV – WHAT YOU NEED TO KNOW?

CHAPTER 7 – THIRTY-SEVEN "MUST KNOW" SALES TERMS

"Genius is 1 percent inspiration and 99 percent perspiration."

– Thomas Edison

The individual recorder holder for US patents, 1,093

If it is good enough for Thomas Edison, it is good enough for you. Here is your homework! Get to know these terms backward and forward. If you are going to interview for a sales position, and you want to be a salesperson, these terms are common sales jargon and are "must know" terms if they are not familiar to you already. The terms are divided into three sections: sales terms, sales jobs terms, and business terms.

Sales Terms

1. Client List
(Also: "Book of Business," "Accounts," or "Customers")

Definition: A salesperson's list of accounts and prospects.
Illustration: "You will take over an excellent client list."
Commentary: The client list you will be responsible for is the lifeblood of any salesperson. Having a well-established client list can provide an excellent opportunity for success with the products or services that you will be selling. If possible, it is worth understanding as much as you can about the top accounts and the opportunities (or challenges) that are present.

2. Cold Calling

Definition: The process by which a salesperson calls a list of prospects who are not expecting the call in an attempt gain an appointment and eventually win their business.
Illustration: "Do you like cold calling?"
Commentary: The interviewer might as well ask if you want to be in sales. Seriously, it is the ability to pick up the phone to create a compelling reason for a buyer to learn more about your products or services. All salespeople must embrace the fact they must be willing to contact people that they, or their company, does not have a relationship with. Some sales positions require more and some require less cold calling.

3. Elevator Pitch

Definition: A well-practiced, short (the length of an elevator ride) description of your product, service, and/or company that is easy to understand and creates interest so the audience wants to learn more.

Illustration: "What is your company's elevator pitch?"

Commentary: The question translates to, "Tell me about your company but don't bore me with details that I won't understand." This description should roll off your tongue quickly without hesitation. The real goal of any elevator pitch is to get the audience interested enough to say, "I get it. Please tell me more."

4. FUD (Fear, Uncertainty & Doubt) – Pronounced "fud"

Definition: FUD is an acronym used to describe how salespeople use fear, uncertainty, and doubt to create a sense of urgency and action about the products or services they are representing.

Illustration: "How much would it cost your company in consulting hours to have your network down and then rebuilt?" I gave that FUD line to the director of technology to get my appointment bragged the salesperson.

Commentary: The sales representative shared information that made the decision maker think that he or she would miss an opportunity or potentially put his or her company at risk. Salespeople often use this tactic when the buyer's perception of the product or service is that it does not require urgent attention today but could result in an emergency if left unattended. In the example, the salesperson might be selling "hacker" intrusion detection software. The director of technology may not have had a problem to date, but if there were a hacker attack tomorrow, the company could have an issue if their intrusion detection strategy is left unmonitored.

5. Good Cop/Bad Cop

Definition: A term taken from the interrogation measures of police who are trying to get information from a suspect in which one police officer assumes a confrontational and derogatory role while another tries to play the role of a confidant to get information from the suspect.

Illustration: "The buyer and his boss play 'good cop/bad cop' with me."

Commentary: This is an easily recognizable strategy when you know about this negotiating tactic. You can diffuse it by pointing out that you recognize the strategy to those people who are involved. I once said with a smile, "What are you guys doing...good cop/bad cop?" They actually replied with a laugh, saying, "No, just bad cop/bad cop." Their attitudes did change for the better after I addressed the issue, and it became one of my best accounts.

6. Hunter-Farmer Sales Team

Definition: A sales team in which one salesperson, the hunter, works to find and cultivate new customers while another (usually an *inside salesperson* – the farmer) will be responsible for "harvesting" the new opportunities that were created by the hunter.

Illustration: "We use the hunter-farmer strategy to work our territories and to maximize our efficiencies."

Commentary: The hunter-farmer sales terminology is used to keep the *outside salesperson* on the road and in front of customers while the farmer can maintain daily contact and support. The farmer position is typically a salesperson in training who will eventually assume the role of a hunter at some point after the on the job training of working directly with a hunter has taken place. The farmer can also be titled *inside sales* or customer service.

7. Open-ended Questions
(Also: "High-gain Questions")

Definition: It is the process by which the salesperson asks a question that cannot be answered with a yes or no answer (closed-ended) but seeks an opinion or statement from the buyer.

Illustration: "What are the issues that the current process creates?"

Commentary: The most important, sometimes the hardest, thing for new salespeople is to be silent and let the buyer answer. In every industry, there are standard "high-gain" questions that salespeople will want to ask on prospecting sales calls to gather information and understand how "real" the opportunity is. Often, sales teams will write down and/or discuss their favorites formally or informally.

8. Product Line(s)
(Also: "Lines")

Definition: The "product lines," as used as a sales term, are the different products and services that a salesperson represents, which may include many different manufacturers and products if he or she is an *independent representative*.

Illustration: "May I schedule some time next Tuesday to meet with you to review some of my new product lines."

Commentary: The "product lines" are what the salesperson is selling. This becomes more complicated when the salesperson is an *independent salesperson* because the list could change weekly. If you work for one specific manufacturer, it will not change as much. The product lines are usually distributed in a printed form or via e-mail as electronic collateral. Salespeople often refer to their product lines as their "line cards."

9. Purchase Order Number ("PO#")

Definition: Purchase Order (PO) number is the legal document from the buyer. The number assigned to the order is used to help track what is being shipped to the buyer for his or her inventory system and financial planning.

Illustration: "I will give you a PO today if you can guarantee delivery on Monday."

Commentary: Purchase order numbers are the final step in any sales process for companies that use PO numbers. It is considered the official binding commitment to purchase the product or service. It is the legitimate time for celebration from a sales perspective. Strike that, it is the precursor to the celebration that comes after the product has been shipped (or the service has been performed) and the invoice has been paid. Restated: POs are a good start for a celebration!

10. Sales Forecasts

Definition: A sales forecast is the process in which the salesperson projects the sales for the month, quarter and/or year. Additionally, salespeople may also have to forecast how many new customers they will gain, how many they will lose, and seasonality of sales volume.

Illustration: "Your quota had you selling 100 units, but you are forecasting a 120. What has changed?"

Commentary: It is common for salespeople to dislike forecasting because it is a time-consuming process. The salesperson argues that time spent on forecasting would have been better spent on selling! However, it becomes a necessity for business planning for items such as cash flow, inventory, and manufacturing requirements of the company. Every company has different philosophies and processes associated with forecasting.

11. Sales Quota
(Also: "Sales Plan")

Definition: The sales quota is the sales goal that a sales manager establishes for a salesperson. It may or may not have his or her involvement. The quota could include a sales dollar amount, product quantities, or a mix of both.

Illustration: "I am setting your quota for 103 units. You sold 93 last year. Our division needs to increase our sales by 10 percent."

Commentary: Quotas are established to set expectations for sales dollars and unit sales. Companies and industries that religiously use quotas to manage their salespeople use them as measuring sticks to determine their effectiveness, ability to meet corporate revenue objectives, and to drive sales of new products and services. There are two ways to issue quotas. There is the top-down approach in which managers set their goals and then divide that goal amongst the salespeople. The other is the bottom-up approach in which the salesperson gives their input on what their quota should be.

In general, larger and publicly traded companies tend to have more quota and forecasting requirements because quotas and forecasts roll into financial reporting to investors. Smaller and private companies tend to be less fixated with quotas because of the *opportunity costs* involved for the time spent by sales managers and salespeople.

12. Sales Cycle

Definition: The sales cycle is the sequence of phases that an average customer goes through when buying a product or service.

Illustration: "Where are you in your sales cycle with that account?"

Commentary: The sales cycle becomes the baseline for internal communication with a sales manager about the relationship with a prospect or a customer. There are many different models for sales cycles depending on the company and industry but the flow tends to be very similar in each case. The complete sales cycle starts with the customer's perception of the product (or service) and the company. It then progresses to the customer being able to articulate the perceived value that the product (or service) offers. The final stage would be the customer's decision to buy (or not) the product (or service).

The first sales cycle on which I received formal training was the "Westvaco Sales Cycle." Westvaco has since merged with The Mead Corporation to form MeadWestvaco but its sales cycle has always been with me in the various sales roles that I have held. Many consider the sales cycle as the starting point in the educational process for all new salespeople.

Westvaco Sales Cycle

7.1

Source: The Forum Corporation of North America and Westvaco. Copyright ©1990. Used with Permission.

13. Sales Pipeline
(Also: "Sales Funnel")

Definition: The sales opportunities that are ranked and monitored as a possibility for winning new business with existing customers or new customers.

Illustration: "How strong is your pipeline this month?"

Commentary: The salesperson must estimate his or her forecast for closing business for that month. The term pipeline or funnel is a means by which sales managers and salespeople rank their winnable business opportunities. Like the *sales cycle*, there are many variations to funnel and pipeline definitions. The common steps (in order): Prospect, Qualified, Presentation, Proposal, Negotiation, and Contracting.

In most cases, the salespeople will assign a probability to possibility of closing the opportunities. For example, a prospect whose been contacted and can describe his or her needs that fit with what the salesperson is offering might be given a 5 percent probability times the potential deal size. After the first presentation, if everything goes well, that prospect might receive a 20 percent probability that is multiplied by the potential deal size and so on.

14. SPIF (Sales Performance Incentive Funds)
(Also: "SPIFF" – Special Incentive for Field Force)

Definition: SPIFs are used to create a special financial bonus for salespeople based on some short-term sales objective.

Illustration: "We got a $500 Best Buy gift certificate SPIF for the salesperson who sells the most new products this month."

Commentary: SPIFs focus the salespeople to push product X for some particular reason (i.e., profitability, slow-moving inventory, or the launch of a new product). This is Pavlov's dog theory to selling. By offering money or a bonus, the salespeople will focus on selling that product. SPIFs are commonly used with *channel partners* and resellers since

Sales Pipeline/Sales Funnel

7.2

Sales "Suspects"
into the funnel

1. Prospects
10 totaling $150,000 x 0%=0

2. Qualified Opportunities
7 totaling $200,000 x 5%=$20,000

3. Presentation of Capabilites
4 totaling $175,000 x 10%=$17,500

4. Proposal to Meet Needs
3 totaling $150,000 x 25%=$37,500

5. Negotiations
3 totaling $300,000 x 50%=$150,000

6. Contracting
1 totaling $75,000 x 75%=$56,250

Pipeline Value $281,250

the manufacturer is competing for the salesperson's selling time and focus.

15. "Terms"
(Also: "Terms & Conditions," "T&Cs")

Definition: The use of the word "terms" or "T&Cs" is the legal wording of the contract (usually does not refer to price and delivery time frame of the product or service).

Illustration: "We are still negotiating T&Cs but we agreed on pricing and the delivery time."

Commentary: The most common use of "terms" for simply payment terms. Two percent Net 30 is an example of payment terms, which means the buyer can deduct two percent off the invoice price if he or she pays within the first 30 days of the invoice date. However, "terms and conditions" can have far-reaching legal concerns. Although it is rare, negotiation terms can occasionally kill deals when legal and business egos get involved settling details in contracts.

16. Trial Close

Definition: It is when a salesperson asks an opinion question to get a buying signal to see how close the customer is to buying.

Illustration: "What color car would you prefer?"

Commentary: The "trial close" is a common strategy when salespeople feel they've completed that selling phase and it is time to move to the next phase of the *sales cycle*. The trial close will give the salesperson feedback to see how close customers are to making a decision. In the car illustration above, the responses could vary widely from "Blue" (I am sold on this car.), "Is that your best price?" (I know you are trying to close me. I like this model of car, but I might still shop your price.), or "I am not sold on this model yet." (Show me some other cars.). In each case, the salesperson got the feedback needed to determine where the buyer was in the *sales cycle* and how to proceed with the buyer.

Sales Jobs Terms

17. Channel Partner

Definition: Channel partners are any third-party organizations or representatives that market, sell, or recommend another company's products or services for financial gain. They could be consultants, distributors, retailers, or *independent sales representatives.*
Illustration: "ABC Consulting is a channel partner for us."
Commentary: Companies look for ways to expand their selling efforts, leveraging people who are not on their payroll, and a channel sales strategy is a way to do that. The auto industry is a long-standing example of how manufacturers sell only their products through channel partners—auto dealers. Another example is the software industry. Microsoft sells its desktop products via the retail channel to consumers, and the rest of their products are sold through a *Value Added Reseller (VAR)* and to the small and medium-sized business community.

18. Channel Sales Manager

Definition: The sales position in a company who manages the sales efforts of the *channel partners* on behalf of the manufacturer or service provider.
Illustration: "John is the channel sales manager for us."
Commentary: Managing the sales channel can be a very dynamic role in the sense that the goal is to keep other organizations interested and filled with incentives to keep promoting your company's products or services.

The challenge for channel salespeople is that partners need to be managed closely because their sales agendas change frequently. Microsoft *channel partners* numbering in the thousands are typically small consulting companies whose successes and failures ebb and flow with the economy and Microsoft's products. A senior person with a lot of experience and connections in the industry usually performs the channel sales manager

role. The channel sales manager is responsible for profiling channel partner targets, creation of *sales quotas*, the structure of the financial plan
to keep the partners focused on their products and marketing efforts in
support of the channel's sales.

19. Independent Sales Representative
(Also: "ISO" – Independent Sales Organization)

Definition: The independent sales representative is a third-party individual or organization that sells, in most cases, multiple companies' products or services.

Illustration: "I am an independent sales representative representing
twelve different manufacturers."

Commentary: ISRs are responsible for their *product lines* and strategic
planning since they are in business for themselves. "Commission only" is
the typical payment structure for their services. ISRs are typically senior
salespeople who are willing to take on the risks (and rewards) of running
their own businesses. They usually are steeped in industry knowledge
and connections with an established track record of sales success.

Another large portion of ISRs are "lifestyle" (aka—"part time") salespeople. They are salespeople who want to work only a certain number of
hours in a week or who do not want to work for anyone else.

20. Inside Sales Representative
(Also: "CSR" – Customer Service Representative)

Definition: Inside salespeople are typically junior salespeople or salespeople who have a travel restriction that prevents them from being an
outside salesperson. They perform "farmer" (see definition under Hunter
& Farmer) support, sales and service for certain company accounts or
prospects.

Illustration: "He is my inside sales representative and will be handling
any ordering details or questions."

Commentary: Inside salespeople are the "details" link between the company and the customer. In most cases the inside salespeople are in the home office, so they will be on the cutting edge of product information, shipping details, and order status. Many *outside salespeople* at one time started as inside salespeople. Inside sales provides value training to understand the company and industry procedures and processes.

21. Outside Sales Representative
(Also: "Outside Salespeople", "Field Sales", "Account Executive", "Territory Manager", "Sales Executive", "National Account Representative")

Definition: The outside salesperson is the one who is responsible for managing, growing, and developing a list of accounts or sales volume in a specific geographic area or industry in a face-to-face manner with the customers.

Illustration: "We have fourteen outside sales representatives who cover twenty-three states."

Commentary: OSRs are considered the "quarterbacks." They are the ones who must help set the internal and external expectations for products and services. Their main goal is to help direct the company's resources to maximize profitability. Travel is a large part of the job requirements of this role.

22. Specification Sales

Definition: A sales process in which products and services are marketed, but there is never a physical order placed with the salesperson.

Illustration: "I got my zip code report for my territory, and my product was still selling extremely well."

Commentary: Their goal of specification sales is to change or confirm someone's buying habits. The most recognizable specification sales position is a brand pharmaceutical salesperson. The salesperson's goal is to inform and educate doctors about why his or her drug is better than the competition's when it is launched and during the product's lifecycle. Because a pharmaceutical sales rep never takes an order from a doctor, the number of prescriptions that are filled in the geography (zip codes) that he or she is covering determines the rep's success.

Another example of specification sales is in the paper business. Specification salespeople call on the print production staff at graphic design agencies to discuss paper options for a project and secure the specification of their product to the printer who ends up printing the project.

23. Value Added Reseller (VAR)

Definition: A VAR is common name given to *channel partners* who are authorized to purchase, resell, and service a manufacturer's product(s) as a part of their own product.
Illustration: "Are you guys a VAR for Oracle?"
Commentary: The "value added" portion of the term refers to additional service support beyond just selling the product. It might be maintenance, installation/implementation, customization, or assistance with buying the product(s).

Business Terms

24. Four Ps of Marketing
(Also: "Marketing Mix")

Definition: A concept that states that there are four parts to marketing products (marketing mix) to a certain target market—product, place (distribution), promotion, and price. E. Jerome McCarthy coined the phrase in his book *Basic Marketing,* published originally in 1960.
Illustration: "We failed because we got only three out of the four Ps of marketing right with our product launch."
Commentary: The four Ps are the building blocks of any product's strategy. Each section should be analyzed for the appropriate fit and cor-

relation within the four Ps marketing plan. As a salesperson, you must know the value of all of the Ps for your products and services and how they relate to your competition to be successful at selling.

Product:

Individual goods, *product lines*, or services offered to the consumer. Aspects include appearance, functionality, quality, accessories, features, installation, instructions, service/support, warranty, packaging, and brand value.

Place (Distribution):

Decisions associated with getting the product to the targeted customer. Aspects include market coverage, sales channel, geographical coverage (locations), logistics (transportation), stocking levels, and service levels.

Promotion:

Communicating and selling to the target customers. Aspects include advertising (sales promotion), personal selling, public relations (news releases), sales personnel, media selection, and budget.

Price:

Pricing analysis that accounts for profit margins on the products and services offered. Pricing also must take into consideration a competitor's marketing mix. Aspects include list price, discounts, allowances, financing, coupons, rebates, and leasing options.

25. "Just In Time" Inventory (JIT)

Definition: The manufacturing methodology in which companies order a small amount of inventory to reduce their costs associated with inventory, warehousing, and cash flow.

Illustration: "Since we have gone to a JIT system, we are more flexible and agile with product improvements and enhancements."

Translation: As a JIT vendor, your company will be contractually obligated to provide products in a timely fashion and at a set price. In most cases, your company will face the consequences of punitive damages if your company does not perform.

Michael Dell, for instance, was the leader in the JIT manufacturing philosophy in the computer industry in the early 1980s. Besides his "direct to the customer" sales model, he also had a unique *OEM* strategy for outsourcing everything except the assembly process and requiring his vendors to provide the inventory service. This provided flexibility in building custom computers to their specification without having to forecast how many to build thus reducing the cost of finished goods inventory.

There are many benefits to JIT inventory programs, but complications can arise when supply of JIT products is interrupted. In the case of a natural disaster, a supplier plant fire can shut down a whole production of finished goods if redundancy of supply is not in place. If demand increases substantially, the vendor and the customer can lose selling opportunities if the whole supply chain cannot produce their products to match the additional requirements.

26. Business Model

Definition: The strategic operational plan for your organization that defines your core business philosophies and goals.

Illustration: "Our business model targets companies between $50 million and $750 million in sales."

Commentary: From a sales perspective, the business model includes the desired *market segment* for the company. The salespeople who target these accounts and prospects become very familiar with their unique business challenges. The customer support group is built around this client profile. Grant Thornton, one of the largest accounting firms in the country (that hardly anyone knows except midsized businesses), has built its business model around that middle *market segment*.

27. Market Segment

Definition: The aggregating of prospective buyers into groups (segments) that have common needs and requirements.

Illustration: "Our products target the first-time home buyer market segment."

Commentary: The market segment is the group of customers to target, recognizing that different market segments have different needs. Sometimes the potential of an innovation is unlocked only when targeting a different market segment.

28. Original Equipment Manufacturer (OEM)

Definition: An original equipment manufacturer (OEM) is a company that builds products or components for use in the production of another company's completed product.

Illustration: "We 'OEM' their products."

Commentary: When a company is your OEM partner, it means that they are supplying parts necessary to produce your product. In the automobile industry, there are hundreds of parts that go into manufacturing an automobile. Consequently, hundreds of OEM vendors are required to produce a vehicle. The car buyers will rarely know the names of OEM companies that are providing the airbags, windshields, and dashboards, for example.

29. Opportunity Costs

Definition: The analysis involved in pursuing one activity or investment instead of another.

Illustration: "After reviewing the opportunity costs of partnering with them, we decided it was worth the effort to hire David to foster the relationship."

Commentary: Opportunity cost, like *ROI*, is analysis to determine how to spend your time, energy, and money associated with an activity versus doing something else. People make these types of decisions and prioritizations every day in business. Salespeople weigh the time and costs spent traveling to remote accounts versus making multiple calls on accounts that are more concentrated in another location.

To provide an example of opportunity costs that a student would appreciate, it is best to use the party vs. study illustration. A similar one was one used by my economics professor. I will never forget it because is it was pertinent to me at the time. Imagine that your tightwad roommate offers you a free ticket to the big concert for that evening at dinner. The problem is you have a test the next morning at 8:00, and you were planning to study that night after dinner. Your decision involves calculating opportunity costs. The probability of a lower grade (cost) on the test is weighed against the enjoyment of going to the concert for free.

30. Product Life Cycle

Definition: The stages in which a product is developed, introduced, grown, matured, and eventually declines or is withdrawn from the market.

Illustration: "We are in the growth phase of our product life cycle."

Commentary: The product lifecycle occurs for every product. Some offerings have a long and extensive time period in all phases of the life cycle while others can go through the phases in a couple of years. Please see the Product Life Cycle, which has been combined with the *Rate of Adoption Curve* in Figure 7.3 for an example of how the product life cycle should be a consideration for salespeople.

31. Rate of Adoption Curve

Definition: The means by which buyers will embrace a new product, service or concept as illustrated in Figure 7.3

Product Life Cycle Combined with the Rate of Adoption Curve

7.3

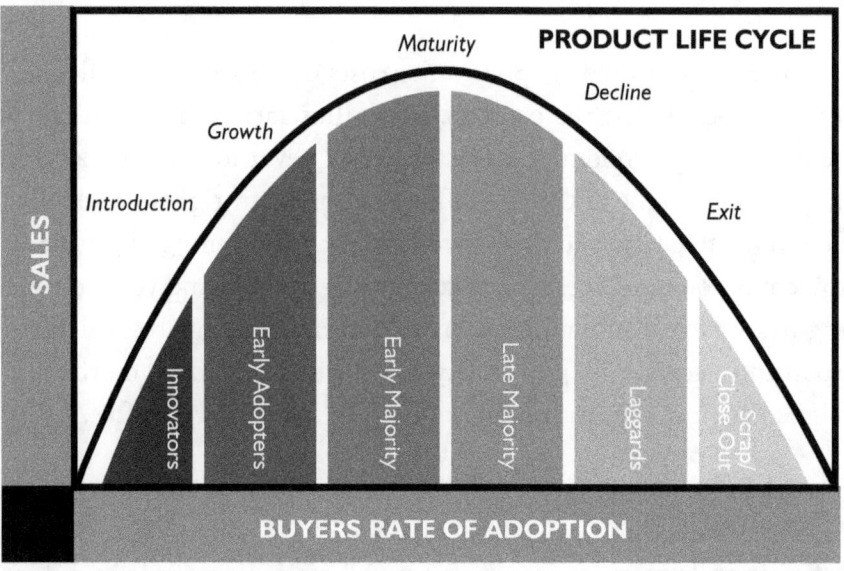

Illustration: "I think we have a good chance at selling them since their key decision maker is an "innovator."

Commentary: The rate of adoption curve is a very useful visual sales crutch to understand why you will not sell every person and company on your first visit if you are selling a new product or service.

Some confident salespeople will take the approach that if the product or service that he or she is selling is that new and innovative this chart becomes irrelevant because of the business value of the product or service. There should not be a "laggard" since the *ROI* will drive a quick decision. The conclusion for the unsuccessful salesperson is that he or she has not done a good enough job getting the *ROI* message across to the buyer. My belief is that a good salesperson can aid in shortening the time axis but you cannot change the buying habits of people and companies.

- Innovators – People and companies leading change.
- Early Adopters – Thought leaders who are willing to accept new ideas and products. They want to be a part of the "leading edge," not the "bleeding edge."
- Early Majority – Careful but ahead of most for accepting change.
- Late Majority – People who accept new products after the majority has embraced them.
- Laggards – People who are accepting of new ideas only after they have become mainstream.

32. Reverse Auctions

Definition: A procurement system used to auction commodity products and services in which vendors bid in real time to obtain business by driving vendor pricing down with each bid.

Illustration: "We continued to bid on the reverse auction until we got to the point where the next bid was below our cost."

Commentary: One of the growing challenges for businesses and salespeople, alike, is online "reverse auctions" for business-to-business (B2B) buying decisions. During his tenure at GE, Jack Welch, at one point, mandated it as a means to procure products at GE. The policy was relaxed because of GE's need to partner on the design aspect of the parts they were buying from their vendors and they were not satisfied with the design teams who were winning the auctions.

It is important to monitor auction trends in the industries you are interested in since it will affect your sales efforts in the future. If it is hard to differentiate your product or service from your competition (a commodity), the chances are good that your customers will be putting your business up for auction.

In essence, they are good for lowering prices, but reverse auctions have a debilitating effect on vendors. The lowest-cost producer will win in an auction setting. A reverse auction minimizes companies that have product feature advantages or intangible value-added services that complement the products on sale. The low-cost producer will continue to follow the pricing down until they win the auction.

33. RIF (Reduction in Force) – Pronounced "Riff"

Definition: It is a term used to describe a structured layoff due to a company's poor financial situation or merger, or as a response to a change in business strategy.

Illustration: "They are expecting a huge RIF a few months after the merger is finalized."

Commentary: Although layoffs are not common with sales positions, they can and will occur when a company is merged or if a company has financial problems. In the pharmaceutical industry, a company might have a RIF of salespeople from a strategy perspective when a large brand drug loses its patent protection earlier than expected because a generic company wins a patent challenge and begins to market its generic version of the brand product. The need for those brand salespeople is eliminated if the company does not have another brand product in the pipeline for those salespeople to market to the doctors.

In 2000, a RIF actually affected me. I was working for a VC backed software company that melted down during the dot-com bust. My wife was five months pregnant with our first child, so it could have been "doom and gloom" if we'd let it. I took the opportunity to completely review my career possibilities (using the concepts of this book)! I revaluated what industry and companies I wanted to interview with and pursue. Fortunately, good sales skills transfer well; I was able to select the industries, companies, and positions that I wanted to pursue. I received five offers in thirty days after my RIF experience.

34. ROI (Return on Investment)

Definition: It is the analysis done to understand why a company might invest dollars (and time in some cases) in an initiative to make money, save money, or meet a business objective.

Illustration: "I know the cost to attend the trade show is $3000, but how can we calculate an ROI for the show?"

Commentary: In the literal sense, it is a finance term. The term was borrowed from the finance department to justify why a company might do or acquire something to determine value. In a sense, you do it every day whether you know it or not on things you buy or how you spend your time. Should I "super size" my meal or just get the $1 burger and water? You analyze the dollar costs and estimate the additional enjoyment and value of the fries and the Coke.

In business, departments other than finance have adopted it to provide a methodology for making fiscally responsible business decisions. A simple example might be when the sales department decides whether to attend a conference. The actual dollar expenses include trade show expense, travel costs, and meal costs. The *opportunity costs* of doing other things also comes into play. The costs will be weighed against the benefits of who (companies and contacts) will be attending the conference, how many new "deals" might be possible from attending, and the negative perception if we don't attend. After analyzing the variables, it will determined that participating in the show will be a positive (go) or negative (don't go) decision.

35. Supply and Demand

Definition: This economic term states that in free markets the price is established by the amount of supply (competitors) versus the amount of buying demand for that product (or service).

Supply and Demand:
Supply Increases, Price Drops

7.4

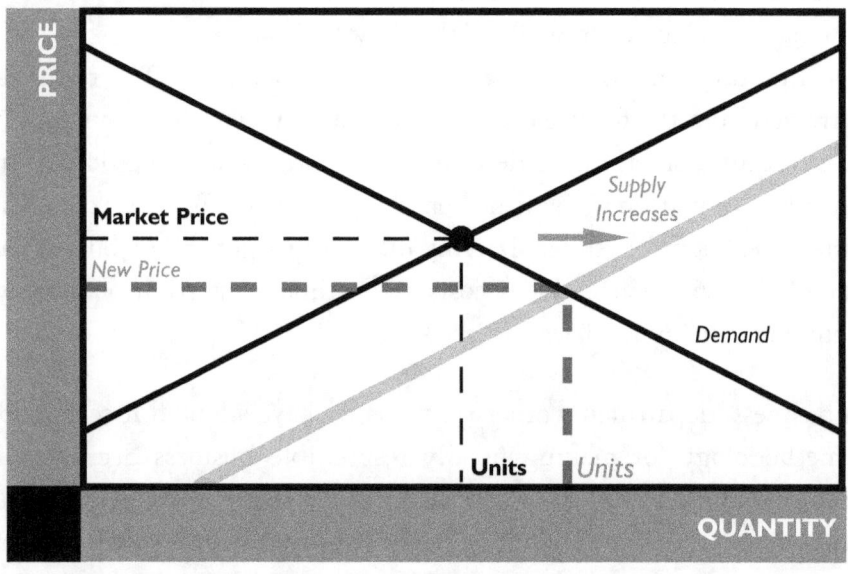

Illustration: "With more manufacturers producing the item, the laws of supply and demand say that pricing must be affected without the demand changing."

Commentary: Any salesperson should know this basic term. Buyers are keenly aware of this term. They like finding other sources for your product since it usually means a lower price for them. Business owners try various ways to differentiate their products or services so the supply and demand principle does not apply to them. Figure 7.4 illustrates a simple supply and demand curve in which there has been an increase in production of product without an increase in the market demand. The result is a lower price in the market.

SWOT Analysis

7.5

| STRENGTHS | WEAKNESSES |
| OPPORTUNITIES | THREATS |

36. SWOT Analysis – Pronounced "Swat"
(Strengths, Weaknesses, Opportunities, Threats)

Definition: The analysis process in which the participants assess the situation, product, service, or entity from their perspective to determine a future strategy or objective.

Illustration: "We need you to do a SWOT analysis on that product line."

Commentary: The SWOT analysis is a very useful strategy tool for outlining and organizing the pros and cons of doing just about anything. It is a very effective tool in a group brainstorming sessions to spur discussion.

I have used it for evaluating everything from government regulations, competition, launching new products, and new job opportunities. I even had to do one on myself for my own yearly performance review.

37. Value Proposition (Value Prop)

Definition: It is how a company would describe its solution to a business' or consumer's problem.

Illustration: "She described her value proposition as helping us to eliminate the raw material waste on our paper machines with the use of her laser strobe."

Commentary: The value proposition, simply, is why the company is in business. It is the critical need the organization's product or service fills for its customers for economic gain. In the illustration above, the product saves the company X amount of money in raw material costs to produce its products, which adds profit to the bottom line. To think of it another way, it is a way to describe your *ROI* to your customers.

CHAPTER 8 – RECOMMENDED READING

"Education has produced a vast population able to read but unable to distinguish what is worth reading."

– G.M. Trevelyan

English historian (1876–1962)

Recommended Reading for Future Salespeople

In "distinguishing what is worth reading," my list of books below gives the reader a focused selection of my favorite books and authors for your consideration. You will recognize some of them already. Some you may have already read since they have been best sellers. I hope you will research the ones you have not heard of by visiting your favorite bookstore, online retailer, or library. I hope they become helpful in furthering your career and personal development.

Personal Development

The 7 Habits of Highly Effective People. Stephen R. Covey, 2004 (15th Anniversary Edition)
How to Win Friends & Influence People. Dale Carnegie, 1981
Wooden. John Wooden, 1997
Who Moved My Cheese? Spencer Johnson, M.D., 1998
Purpose Driven Life. Rick Warren, 2002
Talent is Never Enough, John C. Maxwell, 2007

Business Thought Leadership

Crossing the Chasm. Geoffrey A. Moore, 2002
The One to One Future. Don Peppers and Martha Rogers, PH.D, 1996
Rules for the New Economy. Kevin Kelly, 1999
The World is Flat. Thomas L. Friedman, 2006
Jump Start Your Marketing Brain. Doug Hall, 2004

Selling

Little Red Book of Selling. Jeffery Gitomer, 2004
Selling to VITO. Anthony Parinello, 1999
Solutions Selling. Michael T. Bosworth, 1994

SECTION V – YOUR SALES CAREER STRATEGY CHECKLIST

"In preparing for battle, I have always found that plans are useless, but planning is indispensable"

– Dwight D. Eisenhower

The thirty-fourth President of the United States and a former five-star General in the United States Army

Section I – Why Sales as a Career for You?

Determine if Sales is for You

- Talk to three respected business people who know you well about your interest in sales and get their opinion of your interest in getting into sales.
  - Neighbors
  - Parents' friends
  - Coaches
  - People from your place of worship
- Take a personality profile for your own self-assessment
  - Contact your school's guidance counselors
  - Search online for a personality profile
- Write down your professional goals
  - What is the end goal? Your ambitions?

STOP: Assess the results of your research and analysis. Is a sales career a match for your goals?

Section II – Which Sales Position Is for You?

Evaluate the Industry

- Research the three most appealing Industries to you.
  - Pros and Cons of each (as in Fig. 5.1)
    - What types of sales positions are there?
    - Product or a Service?
    - Growth or Mature?
    - Culture?
    - How are the salespeople valued?

STOP: Are the industries still of interest to you after your research? Eliminate the ones from your list that are not a fit for you. Go to

the places where these products and services are transacted and observe if possible.

Evaluate the Company

- Research at least three companies from the industries that you are interested in.
    - Pros and Cons of each
        - Public vs. Private
        - Experience you will receive
        - Pressure placed on the salespeople there?
        - Sales or strategic involvement?
        - Training program?
        - Advancement path
        - Financial strength of the organization
        - What is the management's background?
        - Company Culture?

STOP: Which companies came to the top of your list of companies? To better understand your top picks, seek out salespeople who have coverage in your area to discuss their industry and their specific companies. Will they help you network and make introductions to hiring managers for interviews?

Evaluate the Sales Position

- What type of sales position is it? (see Figure 4.1)
    - B2C
    - Missionary, Detailing, Specification
    - Channel I
    - Channel II
    - Professional/Semi-Technical
    - Technically Enhanced
    - Strategic Capital Goods/Service

- What products or services will you be selling?
  - How is it positioned in the market? Brand or Commodity?
- Whom to sell to?
  - What does the customer typically look like?
- Skills that you will learn
  - Training
  - Sales skills
    - Negotiation
    - Proposal writing
    - Contacting
  - Industry skills
    - Technical skills
- Who will you learn from?
  - Your boss
  - Coworkers
  - Your customers
- What is the path for advancement in the company?
- Office environment
  - Geographical location of your office
  - The office building
  - Your office setup
    - Length of commute
    - Working out of your home
  - Sales support staff
    - Administrative
    - Technical support
    - Marketing assistance
    - Inside sales
- Stress Factors
  - Sales Representative turnover factors
    - Strategic value to the organization
  - Company culture and values
  - Travel requirements

- Sales pipeline reviews and reporting
- Cold calling and lead generation
- Testing and training of sales representatives
  o Is there a non-compete clause?
  o What are the legal risks associated with the position?

STOP: Use this list to organize your thoughts to prepare for an interview. Some items will have much greater importance than others. Concentrate on those items during your interview. Your focus when first interviewing with a company is to learn as much as you can about the industry, company and position. I would recommend that you arrived organized but do not show up with a list on your first interview and start asking questions to fill out this checklist. Instead, use it as a checklist after your interview to understand what you do not know yet about the position for subsequent interviews.

What are the dynamics of the jobs you are evaluating that are the most important to you? Are there other sales positions that you should investigate because of your analysis? Even though you may have invested a significant amount of time interviewing for a position, should you eliminate it from your consideration because of the analysis?

Section III – Analyzing Sales Job Offers

Sales Compensation

  o What is the compensation plan?
- Salary
- Bonus
- Commission
- Draw

- o Questions for bonus or commissions
  - How often are they paid?
    - Monthly
    - Quarterly
- o Question for draw plans
  - Is the draw recoverable?
  - Can you convert to straight commission?
- o Other financial concerns
  - Health Plan
    - Medical plan
    - Pharmaceutical
    - Dental
    - Vision
    - Short-term disability
    - Life insurance
  - Stocks
    - Employee stock purchase plan?
    - Stock options?
  - Retirement Planning
    - 401K plan
    - 401K match
    - Pension
  - Vesting Periods
    - Stock Options
    - 401K plans
    - Pension
- o Holiday and vacation days
  - How many?
- o Tuition reimbursement
  - How is reimbursement approved?

STOP: Obviously, your compensation plan is very important to understand. You sales management should be able to share with you how your compensation plan works. Do not disrupt sales management and salespeople with detailed questions about the other benefits. If you have questions about them, ask to speak with someone in Human Resources to better understand your specific benefits questions.

Please visit www.salescareerstrategy.com for this and other sales career forms.

www.ingramcontent.com/pod-product-compliance
Lightning Source LLC
Chambersburg PA
CBHW051525170526
45165CB00002B/613